Powerful. Personal. Profound. In his book *New Normal*, my good friend Pastor John Lindell does a fantastic job of leading readers toward rediscovering the promises of God. Drawing deeply from the story of Joshua, Pastor John addresses real tensions we each face as we pursue godly growth. But instead of fixating on the struggles, he shifts our eyes to the Savior, who has gone before us and conquered the Promised Land. There is a possibility of new life in your story, and this book will help you find that.

—LOUIE GIGLIO
PASTOR, PASSION CITY CHURCH
FOUNDER, PASSION CONFERENCES

John Lindell's book *New Normal: Experiencing God's Best for Your Life* will challenge your status quo in the best sort of way. By unpacking the truths of Scripture and sharing powerful personal stories, John will guide you on a faith-filled journey that has the potential to reshape your future.

—CRAIG GROESCHEL
NEW YORK TIMES BEST-SELLING AUTHOR
SENIOR PASTOR, LIFE.CHURCH

In his newest book, John Lindell takes readers on a dynamic journey charted by the life and legacy of Joshua, one of history's greatest leaders. The principles in the pages of *New Normal: Experiencing God's Best for Your Life* have the power and potential to propel everyone who applies them from the ordinary to the extraordinary. Get ready for a new normal!

—MARK BATTERSON
NEW YORK TIMES BEST-SELLING AUTHOR,
THE CIRCLE MAKER
LEAD PASTOR, NATIONAL COMMUNITY CHURCH

John Lindell's *New Normal* will nourish you like manna in the desert! Tracking Joshua as he led the people of Israel into the Promised Land, this book provides rest for your weary heart and fuel for your journey of faith. There's nothing normal about it—John raises the bar and sets a new standard for experiencing God's best in your life.

—CHRIS HODGES
SENIOR PASTOR, CHURCH OF THE HIGHLANDS
AUTHOR, *THE DANIEL DILEMMA* AND *OUT OF THE CAVE*

Never before in my lifetime have I seen our great, big, beautiful, and broken world this desperate for a new, more hopeful kind of normal. And rarely before have I met a leader more effective than Pastor John Lindell when it comes to being the proverbial straw through which our Creator-Redeemer breathes life back into dry bones. I'm a huge fan of everything he writes and preaches, but I think *New Normal: Experiencing God's Best for Your Life* may just be his best message yet. Revival, here we come!

—LISA HARPER
SPEAKER AND AUTHOR, *THE SACRAMENT OF HAPPY*

God's plan for our lives is always more than we think or imagine. Stepping out of a comfortable season into where God is leading helps us discover this. Pastor John's timely encouragement to make the decision to walk by faith and experience all that God offers from it is much needed. *New Normal* will encourage you to take that next step out of the familiar and into God's next season for you and will teach you how not to miss all that God is currently doing in your life. I pray that *New Normal* brings you new perspective and a closer relationship with God as He leads you.

—CHAD VEACH
LEAD PASTOR, ZOE CHURCH LA

NEW NORMAL

JOHN LINDELL

CHARISMA
HOUSE

Visit the author's website at jamesriver.church and newnormalbook. org.

Library of Congress Cataloging-in-Publication Data:
An application to register this book for cataloging has been submitted to the Library of Congress.

International Standard Book Number: 978-1-62999-910-4
E-book ISBN: 978-1-62999-911-1

21 22 23 24 25 — 987654321
Printed in the United States of America

TO DEBBIE, MY BEAUTIFUL BEST FRIEND.
YOUR LOVE HAS MADE MY LIFE FULL—
YOUR JOY HAS MADE IT FUN.

CONTENTS

Foreword by Brian Houston xiii

Prologue xvii

1 Strength Training 1

2 More Heart 19

3 Setting Yourself Up for a Miracle 39

4 Thanks for the Memories .57

5 Letting Go 71

6 Seeing What God Sees 87

7 Praise That Paves the Way 107

8 The Law of First Things .121

9 Asking for Directions 135

10 Crazy-Big Requests 147

11 Full-On 157

12 Living for Legacy 167

Epilogue 177

Acknowledgments 181

Notes 183

FOREWORD

JOHN AND I met around twenty years ago in Kansas City. In all that time, his devotion to loving God and loving people has remained fervent—qualities that have shaped him into a great friend and pastor. He has led James River Church alongside his wife, Debbie, for nearly three decades, and together they have built a thriving church. The insight in this book stems from the fruit of his life, which has been entirely dedicated to the cause of Christ and helping others step into their God-given potential.

There has never been a more imperative time to be aware of the reality that we are not solely citizens of this world but more importantly citizens of heaven and children of God through faith in Jesus Christ. In *New Normal*, John proclaims a timely reminder that the boundaries of the lands and frontiers we are called to occupy are not created by human hands but authored by a generous and loving heavenly Father, who desires to bless His children.

God has a spacious life planned for you that is full of His goodness and blessing. The enemy would love nothing more than to put a question mark over the goodness of God in your life and trick you into thinking and believing small, stunting your ability to see the wonder and possibility of a bright future. The apostle Paul emphasized this in his letter to the Corinthian Church:

> Dear, dear Corinthians, I can't tell you how much I long
> for you to enter this wide-open, spacious life. We didn't
> fence you in. The smallness you feel comes from within
> you. Your lives aren't small, but you're living them in
> a small way. I'm speaking as plainly as I can and with
> great affection. Open up your lives. Live openly and
> expansively!
>
> —2 CORINTHIANS 6:11–13, MSG

We can all be drawn into thinking small, but John will inspire you to live expansively, extending the limits of what seems possible to experience God's blessing in ways you never could have imagined.

Many of us misunderstand what it means to be blessed because we are simply unaware of the full story. It begins with God creating humanity, humanity rebelling against God, humanity attempting to rescue themselves, and then God choosing a man named Abraham through whom He would initiate saving the world. God declares His blessing to Abraham in Genesis 12:1–3 (NLT):

> Leave your native country, your relatives, and your
> father's family, and go to the land that I will show you.
> I will make you into a great nation. I will bless you and
> make you famous, and you will be a blessing to others.
> I will bless those who bless you and curse those who
> treat you with contempt. All the families on earth will
> be blessed through you.

God chose to bless Abraham purely because He desired to, not because of anything Abraham did or could do to earn it. God's blessing says more about Him than it does about us—it is not given based on performance or achievement but because it is part of God's unchanging nature to bless His children. Abraham received God's blessing by faith, and because of this we can too. Jesus is referred to as the "seed of Abraham" (Gal. 3:16, 29, NIV), and it is through faith in Jesus Christ that we become heirs of God's blessing. And while God's blessing has already been lavished upon those who are in Christ, it is important to recognize that we are blessed by both faith *and* obedience. God instructed Abraham to *go*, and on the other side of his obedience to leave his native country was new territory and great blessing.

The story of God's blessing continues to unfold in your life. If you hunger for more of God and crave a richer, deeper, and more fulfilling existence, I believe the wisdom and biblical insight within this book will pump fuel into your engine for the road ahead. If you believe you are blessed, then today is the day to start living it.

Don't be surprised if you encounter opposition just as you start to pursue your promise—as you take ground, the enemy loses ground. The Bible describes Caleb as having a "different spirit" (Num. 14:24), one that caused both him and Joshua to see possibility where others saw challenge, and opportunity where others saw obstacles. A priority of safety will keep you where you are—but when God places a longing in your heart for something more, will you trust that He will lead you to discover it?

New Normal will stir and awaken your spirit to the reality that there is a promised land full of God's goodness and blessing, and it is worth the risk to follow God's guiding hand all the way there. I love what John has written about this:

We spend much of our lives believing we are outside His blessing looking in but never knowing a sustained experience of God's best. Our acquaintance with the fullness of God's goodness is sporadic because we are not willing to wage the battle necessary to inhabit that new normal.

Strength and courage will be required to occupy the land—but God is with you, and His blessing is both upon and before you. My friend John has penned this book with you in mind, and my prayer is that you will consume the wisdom in every chapter and that you will be greatly encouraged as you wholeheartedly dive into this resource.

Be blessed, stay strong, and enjoy the journey. God is on your side!

—BRIAN HOUSTON
GLOBAL SENIOR PASTOR, HILLSONG CHURCH

PROLOGUE

Moses my servant is dead. Now then, you and all these people, get ready to cross the Jordan River into the land I am about to give to them—to the Israelites.

JOSHUA 1:2 | *NIV*

THE SUN WAS just starting to go down behind him, sweet relief from the unfiltered heat of a big Middle Eastern sky. Joshua felt the sticky mud against his sandals as he walked closer to the river, the banks saturated by high waters during flood season. For the moment, he could take in the wild beauty of the Jordan. But the snakelike zigzag of the river wasn't just a beautiful backdrop; it was a boundary—the end of the world as he knew it. His people had spent a long time wandering in the wilderness. Still, for all the frustration and occasional boredom of those barren years, there was a certain familiarity and predictability to them too. You can get used to anything, even the wilderness, and you find a certain comfort and routine in dealing with the devil you know.

For many of the younger Israelites the far side of the Jordan might as well have been the other side of the moon, as they only knew about the land on the other side through stories. But Joshua knew the land in a first-person, experiential way that had ignited his dreams every night since he was a very young man. Young Joshua had been one of twelve men sent by the legendary Moses to spy on the Canaanite nations and report back the agriculture and lay of the land. The other men who had gone with him brought back an unbalanced report, full of terror, teeth chattering as they talked about the fortified cities and powerful people they saw.

But Joshua and his companion Caleb had seen more than the obstacles: They saw that the land flowing with milk and honey they had heard legends about was not a myth but a reality. They saw lushness, and they saw a land full of fruit, a land full of opportunity. But more than that, because they believed in the God of the Hebrew people, they saw a land of promise because they saw the land through the lens of faith.

> **You can get used to anything, even the wilderness, and you find a certain comfort and routine in dealing with the devil you know.**

When all the other spies had said the challenges were too great and too many, Joshua and Caleb were the ones who had silenced the quivering voices of fear and said, "We should go up and take possession of the land, for we can certainly do it." When everybody else said it could not be done, they were the counterwitnesses who said, "It *must* be done, and we are the only ones who can do it." They had seen the Promised Land, felt the carpet of grass beneath their feet, tasted the air in their mouths, and felt the possibility and even necessity deep in their guts.

They had been to the Promised Land as visitors. And if you're honest, you probably have been too. The promised land has always been a major tourist attraction for daydreamers. Many people imagine a land of promise, opportunity, adventure, risk, taking God at His word, and living from a deep sense of purpose. And yes, many people will visit or perhaps even vacation there. It's a safe enough proposition to put your toe over the boundary of a place you have not been to, risking just enough to feel the breeze of a different kind of place and imagine yourself in a different kind of life. But most people go back home after the vacation. Most people wake up after the dream. Most people who visit the land decide that living there would not be practical or pragmatic. It's one thing to visit the promised land, to go on a sightseeing trip. But could you take the risk of living there?

Even after all the years that had passed, Joshua could not let go of the things he saw and felt when he stepped onto the land. He could not forget the faith and fire he felt in his bones. He had never let go of his dream of crossing over into a different place, a land of promise, a different kind and quality of life. He never let go of the promise, and the promise never let go of him.

Every once in a while, along comes a woman or man who won't let go of the dream, a person who is not content just to visit the land. Something pushes them to explore the place no one else is willing to explore. Sometimes it's as simple as refusing to ignore the itch you can't quite ever scratch, that sometimes dormant but ever-present desire for something *more*. There is no promotion, no relationship, no house that can fulfill that nagging sense that you are built for something deeper, richer, and fuller. Complacency, fear of the unknown, or any number of things keep most people from ever seriously considering crossing over into the land. But for some the restlessness is too great.

For others the catalyst for this new exodus—this transition, this crossing over—is tragedy. Joshua knew the restlessness, but he knew about loss too. Moses had died, and his death marked not just the end of a legend but the end of an era. Similar to the way people can tell you where they were when JFK got shot or when they first got the news about 9/11, for Joshua's people, Moses' death was a shattering event that changed everything. But unlike so many of his contemporaries, Joshua didn't just grieve the end of

Moses the way you grieve some mythological folk hero; he had walked close enough to Moses to grieve the death of a man he loved.

Joshua had been Moses' assistant, and that arrangement had always been more than enough for him. He loved his mentor too much to envy him. His proximity to Moses gave him more reverence for the mystery of his life, not less. He saw the miracles. He saw him walk under the weight of an all-consuming call. By all accounts Moses was the greatest man to ever come from his people, and Joshua was more than satisfied to walk in the shadow of his extraordinary life. He had no need or desire to be "the guy." Joshua had known his role as Scottie Pippen to Moses' Michael Jordan, and he had been fully satisfied with it.

Besides, a man like Moses was a generational phenomenon. A military genius in his own right, Moses also happened to be the man who won a staring contest with Pharaoh. He told the most powerful man in the world to let his people go, saw the Red Sea part when he lifted his famous staff, and brought the Ten Commandments down from Mount Sinai, where, amid the thunder and lightning, he caught a glimpse of the living God and somehow lived to tell about it. Like with all saints, Moses' exploits and stories only seemed greater when they were retold after his death. Even his stutter became the stuff of legend. But Joshua knew Moses before the glory of God shone on his face; he loved him then, and he loved him when the shine wore off too. He didn't just lose a folk hero, an *idea* of Moses; he lost a father figure and a friend. Nothing was ever the same after that.

Sometimes this is the way it happens: you stay where

you've always been until tragedy displaces you and moves you forward. Moses' death was the catalyst for a new chapter in Israel's story, and the news that threatened to break Joshua down was now breaking him open to a new word from God: *it's time to cross the Jordan.* It's time to stop living in the past and live a new story. It's time to stop walking in circles and go walking into a new land.

I'm wondering where you are reading this and what river you know you are being called to cross over. I'm wondering what you are staring into right now—what place you've never been before, what challenge you've never faced. If you're like most people, part of your life has been spent in some kind of wilderness, walking in circles, turning around at the same dead ends. And yet, as Moses' death was for Joshua, maybe something is shifting in you and you know it's time to come into an undiscovered discovery.

It's not because you are ambitious but because there is some new land you know God is calling you to occupy. There is some new place where you know you have to go spiritually, emotionally, and maybe even geographically. God's promise is always a promise of *land*—of dirt and soil, of place, of ground beneath your feet. It's a particular place with a particular people, where you stop just living a story that you inherited or a story that has been given to you. You start living a story of your own, walking in faith that becomes your faith, following a God who wants to be known as *your* God.

What do you feel in your bones when you look across the river Jordan? Can you taste the fear in the back of your throat, or maybe even the adventure? Does your stomach get butterflies at the thought of it, or does it drop to the floor altogether? Crossing over into new land can be a scary thing, and all the more when "Moses" is dead—the support system you used to have doesn't support you anymore, the faith that used to be enough is too small to sustain you now, or the person you relied on isn't here for you anymore.

As Moses' death was for Joshua, maybe something is shifting in you and you know it's time to come into an undiscovered discovery.

But the land was also called "promised" for a reason: It flowed with milk and honey. It was teeming with goodness, hope, and possibility. For whatever else might make you afraid, have you suspected that there is a God who is for you and not against you, who would do anything to bless you, to care for you and yours, to help you come into this new place? Maybe you have sensed the fear. But have you sensed the potential? Have you felt the longing? Because God is calling you to a good place, a hopeful place, a beautiful place where there is love, victory, and community—a place you can finally call home. Have you ever felt the ache for such a place?

Joshua felt it all that afternoon, watching the sun slowly start to dip into the waters. He felt the ache for Moses, the man he revered. He felt nostalgic. The fear and the adrenaline, the excitement at what was ahead, were indistinguishable in his body. He did not know what the journey would look like or precisely what it would demand of him. What he knew was that there was no going back to where he started; there was no turning around. Whatever else might lie ahead, this part was certain: he would have to cross this river right in front of him. Whether or not the rising waves of the river parted now as they did for Moses, there was no going back. He didn't know what manner of life awaited him on the other side, only that he would have to cross over to have any meaningful life to live at all.

Not being a man given to delusions of grandeur, Joshua had not lived his life with a sense of destiny on his shoulders. He still couldn't believe the voice that called out to Moses in the wild was now calling his name. But he knew deep in his belly that he heard the voice for himself, that something undeniable was calling him to cross over to the other side.

There was so much about the undomesticated world stretching out in front of Joshua to be afraid of, yet the voice told him with relentless consistency, "Don't be afraid." The voice kept telling him to be strong and courageous in a time when he felt anything but. Joshua knew he had to go because there was more at stake than just his own future—his destiny was connected to that of the people around him. "Now proceed to cross the Jordan, you and all this people, into the land that I am giving to them, to the Israelites" (Josh. 1:2, NRSV). What will you do with this stirring that you feel? This holy restlessness has implications for your husband or your wife, your kids, your friends, and the broader story of the people around you.

And while there may yet be particular places you are called to explore in this new land, there is something wonderfully open-ended about it all too. "Every place that the sole of your foot will tread upon I have given to you" (v. 3). Did you see that? *Every* place. Anyplace you go. A few verses later the promise is that "you may have good success wherever you go" (v. 7). Don't skip over the wide-open space in the word *wherever*. There is something about crossing over that has to do with finding your sense of agency, your voice. You aren't called to be a mere passive spectator in a scripted plot but, according to the apostle Paul, God's fellow worker. (See 1 Corinthians 3:9.) You get to create, explore, and partner with God in making up this new story.

Still, no matter how tantalizing the promise, it doesn't negate the fact that it's terrifying to consider crossing into a land where you've never been before, trusting God in a way you never have before, in a country where your GPS doesn't work. It's one thing to read about Bible characters' great exploits, but your life is not a vacation Bible school. And hey, after all—you are no Moses. Really, who is?

Joshua felt it too—the unworthiness, the anxiety. Moses was the Rolling Stones; Joshua had a band in his garage. He was all too aware of his humanity. Yet as often as he felt fear begin to rise, the word of the Lord kept coming to him over and over: "Be strong and courageous. Do not be frightened, and do not be dismayed, for the LORD your God is with you wherever you go" (Josh. 1:9). And why did the voice tell him to be strong and courageous? Because Joshua did not always feel strong and courageous. Why did the voice tell him not to be frightened or dismayed? Because crossing over could be frightening, and the wildness of life on the other side of the "uncrossable" river could have been reason enough to make him feel dismayed.

God kept saying it over and over, every time Joshua remembered the reasons to be afraid. Time and time again, for every fear that surfaced, the words would come rushing back: "the LORD your God is with you wherever you go" (v. 9).

The breeze rolled onto Joshua softly off the river as the sun was completing its final descent into the water. Feeling the wind on his face, hearing the soft rustle of it in the brush, he saw his lone, solitary shadow reflecting on the surface. But he knew in his very bones on the eve of crossing over that he was anything but alone.

And neither are you.

Start Somewhere

What if that which you have grown accustomed to is far less than what God has for you? What if what you call normal falls tragically short of what you were created for? What if the only difference between living in God's best and living where you find yourself today is simply your willingness to rise and fight to experience the new normal He has for you?

Far too many of us visit the land of God's blessing but never live there. We spend much of our lives believing we are outside His blessing looking in but never knowing a sustained experience of God's best. Our acquaintance with the fullness of God's goodness is sporadic because we are not willing to wage the battle necessary to inhabit that new normal.

But everybody has to start somewhere. Why not here? Why not now? I don't know what kind of transition you might be in. I don't know what or, like Joshua, *whom* you might have lost. I just know there is a river that needs to be crossed now. And I know there is always a land full of promise and opportunity for God's children who are willing to take the risk of following wherever God leads. What is the river you know you must cross? What is the fear that grips your heart when you think about crossing into that new land? Where is the hope, the sense of promise, the adventure?

Far too many of us visit the land of God's blessing but never live there.

You don't have to know where your story is going. You don't have to know how to get *there*, but you do know you have to start *here*—with this river, this thing right in front of you. Maybe you struggle with feeling unqualified. Fearlessness is not required of you to move forward. Faith is. And faith is not a feeling; faith is an action, a response to what God is calling you to do. Faith doesn't mean your knees don't ever knock. Faith just means you keep on walking ahead even when they do.

Pushed to the Edge

It's a pattern as old as creation itself, but it never gets any easier: something has to die for new life to come. It's the rhythm of all created things, the cycle of life. Moses was the most beloved leader in Israel's storied history—he still is. The people loved him, revered him, and treasured him. They surely would have chosen the comfort of an ailing Moses in any form, so long as he was still alive, so long as he was still present, over the cruel alienation of death. And yet it wasn't until Moses crossed over from this world to the next that the people of God would cross over the Jordan River and thus from the long, ambling, in-between season into the land God intended for them to possess. Something had to end so that something new could begin.

> **It's a pattern as old as creation itself, but it never gets any easier: something has to die for new life to come.**

By nature we are creatures of habit, ordering our lives around routines that give us comfort. From time to time we may glimpse something of a wilder life based on trust rather than certainty, but we tend to visit exotic places rather than live there. We want to go camping but not live in the woods. We want to go on a safari but not live in the jungle. We want to taste the untamed beauty at the edge of the world but then retreat quickly back to the suburbs. We want just enough action to liven things up a little and give us the occasional rush of adrenaline. The whole untethered life of adventure that faith summons us to? Well, that is another thing entirely.

It's rarely within us to *choose* such a thing, so as often as not, we don't. If it were up to us, we'd choose the same old pattern and routine, the same old normal. We'd choose the way it's always been, even if the way it's always been is not great—until life happens to us in some way. Moses dies. Something happens that we could never have prepared for. And at that moment, the invitation comes.

I like routine. I like knowing how the day is going to roll. Having a plan and working a plan is the way I lead. When COVID-19 hit, we were suddenly dealing with whole new realities—and even after spending hours the first few weeks of the pandemic crafting plans, we had to throw them out based on new developments. This pattern recurred, reminding us of the reality that we never know what the future holds. We needed that reminder because the predictability of our precoronavirus world had dulled us to that reality. This understanding didn't lighten the burden of caring for people and stewarding the leadership of the church.

As time went on, however, we found that with this unprecedented season came unprecedented opportunity. It forced us to reimagine how people were engaged with the gospel. It forced us to reimagine how to be a voice of hope and peace during an international crisis. It became an opportunity for weakness to be exposed and new strength to emerge from unexpected places and people. It wasn't a reality that we chose. But in the ending of one season, we recognized the invitation of the Spirit. Something had permanently shifted, and there would be no going back to the world we had known before.

This particular season has marked a global shift in how people think about human connection and intimacy. It has caused us to rethink the necessity (or lack thereof) of working at an office versus working from home. It has redefined how we travel, how connected we are to our neighbors, how fragile our economy is, and how fragile our interconnected ecosystems are. And for a little while many of us couldn't help but muse out loud about how we couldn't wait to get back to the way things were. Yet, as many of us know who have buried a loved one or gone through some kind of trauma—a long-term illness, a devastating breakup, depression, financial collapse—there are some experiences from which there is no going back.

Such is the place in which we now find ourselves. There is no going back to "normal." The world we knew before and the way we knew it before simply does not exist. That job, that relationship, that way we had of looking at the world before we lost someone or something close to us—perhaps simply before we lost that naive sense of stability that things would always go on the same way—is not going to come back.

What if it's not supposed to? What if "normal," even when it's not bad, is precisely where most of us get stuck? The land of normal is neither a place of possibility nor a place of battle; it is a place of false comfort based on an illusion that we are more in control than we really are. The land God calls us to is often wilder and will require more of us. It's full of beauty and wonder too—deeper experiences of faith, deeper revelations of God, more deeply connected relationships, and certainly a deeper sense of fulfillment.

But the risk is higher to enter this promised land, this new normal. If it were a simple matter of sitting down and making a list of pros and cons—"To Enter the Land or Not to Enter the Land"—a lot of us might not seriously consider it because the risk of losing the comfort and routine of what we think we already have seems too great.

That's why I've written this book, which explores the peril and promise of the land. Yes, there are real reasons that most people will decide that it is too risky to leave their driveway for the kind of adventure real faith demands. But without glossing over the land's challenges, I want to show you why you can trust the God who calls you into this new territory, how to start moving toward it from where you are, and what to do once you get there. You will not always know precisely what lies ahead as you walk, but you will come to know that the One who calls you to walk on will be faithful to sustain you. Even though the particulars of our roads will be different, the landscape of any journey into the land is ultimately the same. It's a journey of faith, obedience, and consecration, where only trust can guide us safely through a place riddled with giants we don't know how to fight and walls we don't know how to scale. But with Joshua—and more importantly, the Spirit that whispered to him—as our guide, it is possible not only to explore the land of God's blessing but also to live in it, dwell in it, and build a story and legacy in it. In the pages ahead, Joshua's journey of faith will be our field guide to lead us into the new normal God has for us.

I suspect that you picked up this book because you aren't satisfied with the "normal" you find yourself in, that something in your life has triggered a hunger for more. It often takes something catastrophic to dislodge us, to shake us out of the familiar comfort of the good old normal. That's not to say God directly authors these things—that God directly sends a virus or kills our loved ones or anything like that; the relationship of God's providence to human action is complex and would be a whole different book. But repeatedly in Scripture and the texts of our lives we see that coming to the end of one story opens the possibility of another. Coming to the boundary of one land, to the end of the world as we've known it, takes us to the edge of an undiscovered country where possibility and adventure await.

01

STRENGTH TRAINING

Have I not commanded you? Be strong and courageous. Do not be afraid; do not be discouraged, for the LORD your God will be with you wherever you go.

JOSHUA 1:9 | NIV

NYONE WHO KNOWS me knows I am competitive. Part of the fun of playing is playing to win, and I am willing to push myself as hard as I have to if I believe victory is on the line. But just like anything else, this competitive drive has its potential pitfalls.

A few years ago I felt as if I was getting a little out of shape and knew I needed a new fitness routine, so I signed up for a class called Bootcamp. The name says it all. It was an hour of nonstop intensive cardio, made up of a seemingly unending onslaught of bear crawls, floor sweepers, mountain climbers, push-ups, sit-ups, squat jumps, and anything else my instructor (a.k.a. the drill sergeant) could dream up.

I showed up on the first day to find the gym full of mostly twenty- and thirty-year-olds. At this point I should mention I was turning fifty that year! Undeterred, I decided to prove to myself and everyone else who might be watching that I could win. Unfortunately my long-dormant muscles hadn't gotten the memo! It would be a while before my body could match my competitive drive. After that first session, I felt fine when I left the gym. It wasn't until the next day when I went to get out of bed that my legs, which had pumped so hard the morning before, were too stiff and sore to navigate any incline. Forget climbing stairs; they were off-limits. My desire to compete had backfired. It was obvious that growing stronger would take time and training.

If you're like me, you have had seasons where you have felt compelled to get physically stronger, and that's a good thing. There are real benefits to getting in better shape, from reducing the risk of heart disease or diabetes to managing emotional stress and improving mental health. Still, I can't help thinking that what we go looking for at the gym only scratches the surface of a much deeper longing, a desire for something more primal. After all, so much of life in contemporary America is an indoor sport. Most challenges of our existence only simulate the kind of adventure found in the wild. Humanity—women and men alike—craves the adrenaline that comes from rising to a challenge, living the life of a warrior. Something inside us wants to push outside the boundaries of the world as we've known it, conquer new territory, take new ground in the landscape of the world inside or outside us, and occupy spaces that seem to lie just beyond the limits of attainability. The boundaries that have been drawn for us come to feel too tight and constrictive, and we yearn for a more open space. Yesterday's strength is simply insufficient for where we long to go today. In short, we need to find a new strength for a new normal.

> **Humanity—women and men alike—crave the adrenaline that comes from rising to a challenge, living the life of a warrior.**

Tired of being domesticated by the world in which we control the thermostat and the ding of a new voice mail or tweet controls us, we crave something wilder. It's not the superficial desire for more stuff, more money, more gadgets, or more followers that motivates us—not deep down—but a desire for more life, more wonder, more beauty, and more victory. In our more hopeful moments we have glimpsed that new territory, that land where milk and honey flow.

We have seen a place outside the landscape of mediocrity where we can imagine being free and entering a season of new blessing. But we have also seen giants in that land—and sometimes giants in ourselves. These giants mock our desires, taunt our determination, and intimidate us to stop us from experiencing the personal growth and freedom we desire.

> **It's not the superficial desire for more stuff, more money, more gadgets, or more followers that motivates us—not deep down—but a desire for more life, more wonder, more beauty, and more victory.**

I have no judgment on anyone who wants to get stronger physically. However, I do wonder if much of what happens in the gym is still only an indoor simulation of the kind of adventure our souls crave—of charting out new territories, exploring new lands, living undeterred by and unafraid of the giants that have kept us from finding true strength and real courage and coming into our own kind of promised land.

If something inside you craves that kind of adventure, where you can taste the fear in the back of your throat but decide to press on ahead anyway, I've written this book for you. If something inside you longs for that kind of bravery, unintimidated by any giant and unwilling to accept the boundaries of the world as it's been given to you, then keep reading! No previous feats of strength, mighty acts of valor, battle experience, or special courage is required of you. The only prerequisite is to want, to desire—or even just *the want to want.* If you are willing to consider that God might want you to occupy new land, a new normal, and He will forge within you the strength required to step into what lies on the horizon—even that little bit of openness or desire is more than enough to get you out of the driveway.

If you want to be stronger and want the story of your life to be part of a broader story of victory and triumph, I hope you will take this journey. You'll find yourself standing alongside a brave soul who stood at the precipice of an unexplored, unknown land; saw the giants that inhabited that land; felt the pull of the safe, familiar life he once knew tug on his insides—and yet decided to keep going.

Hitting the Wall

Real change in our lives requires more than just another New Year's resolution. All of us face spiritual resistance to stepping into the land that God is calling us into, because the stakes are considerably higher. That's why all of Scripture frames spiritual growth that results in a physically different life as a battle with ourselves and with spiritual forces of evil. When we get serious about growing in our faith, going deeper in our connection with God, and finding the land God has called us to explore, the resistance will be real, intense, and fierce. No matter how good our intentions are, even the best of us will hit a wall, a challenge that will test our resolve and make us question whether we had any business setting out on this journey in the first place. And no matter how much (or little) you've been to the gym, you will find out very quickly that physical strength simply will not be enough.

Tucked within the Old Testament story of Joshua we

see that the strength a new normal requires is not defined within the typical boundaries of how we seek strength. Not only does God tell Joshua repeatedly not to be afraid, but God also tells him over and over to "be strong and courageous." That's perhaps easier said than done, especially in a world where strength is so ambiguously defined. What exactly does it mean to be strong or to act strong? Is being brave synonymous with big muscles, rigid determination, or utter fearlessness?

On the contrary, we often have our most primal encounter with fear just as God calls us into the new normal. Feeling the fear doesn't necessarily mean you are in the wrong place at the wrong time. It often means you are on the precipice of the new land God is calling you to enter. Sometimes the fear of the unknown is synonymous with the Spirit's invitation into something new that God is doing around you and wants to do in you. It doesn't feel like that in the moment—in fact sometimes it can feel like getting punched in the gut.

Have you ever had a moment that completely took the wind out of your sails or physically knocked the wind out of you? I have. I've lived long enough to have my share of adventures, to enter into some promised land in my life, to see the faithfulness of God in it and feel the courage rise up inside me in response. I've tasted some victories—not because I was strong enough but because God was strong in me.

But I've also had some moments when I felt anything but strong and courageous. I've stood at the start of a new chapter in my life, unsure whether I had what it took to enter that new season. Perhaps you are plagued by self-doubt and insecurity, as many of our biblical heroes were. Or maybe you thought you were strong until, like me, you came to a particular river in front of you—some external obstacle that made you wonder if you could find it inside yourself to keep walking at all.

> **Feeling the fear doesn't necessarily mean you are in the wrong place at the wrong time. It often means you are on the precipice of the new land God is calling you to enter.**

When you do life with people, not only do you grow to love them, but also you come to depend on them. If you're not careful, you can find yourself depending on them more than you depend on God. Several years ago I got some news that brought this very thing to light. I hit a wall that at the time felt as high as the walls of Jericho. This story starts at my bathroom mirror moments after I had received news that a key staff member was resigning. I had become so used to this person fighting life's battles beside me that I didn't feel strong enough to fight them on my own. In that moment it wasn't fear that paralyzed me; it was discouragement.

As I was shaving that morning, I remember seeing my eyes in the mirror and, for the first time, not seeing any fight in them. I had been a pastor all my adult life, and God had already proved Himself faithful through many wins and losses in my time. The church was growing. God had made a way for us through every difficult transition we had experienced, through every experience of breaking new ground and entering a new land. Some part of me knew that God would be faithful again—or, at least, some part of me knew that I was *supposed* to know that!

But this time was different somehow. I had faced other challenges that were just as daunting on the outside, but this time I felt rattled. I felt gut-punched. For the first time in my ministry at James River Church, I had lost my heart for the battle.

At some point in our lives we all find ourselves staring at some new and unfamiliar land God is calling us to take inhabited by some new and unfamiliar enemy. The thrill of the adventure of coming into something new is real, but the threat of the battle is very real too. And when you stand on that precipice, surveying that new land, a little voice inside your head tells you, "You don't have what it takes for this one."

And the voice is not wrong.

Technically speaking, we are never formally qualified to take any new land in our lives. By definition it's a challenge we have not yet faced. It's a moment we have not yet lived. A leap of faith is being required of us that we've not yet made. The fear isn't just in your head—there may not be anything on your résumé that has prepared you for the thing you are facing right now.

As I look back over my life, I realize I have felt unprepared for most of the new normals in my life, even in ministry. I don't come from a minister's family. I've had some wonderful mentors along the way, but no seminary prepared me for the seemingly endless challenges I've faced on the ground in my life as a pastor. Every battle is easier to fight when you feel strong. As I stood there looking in the mirror, I felt a complete absence of strength.

But then, there was another voice, quieter than the one reverberating in my head telling me I wasn't up for the challenge this time. This one was still and small, but distinct, recognizable. This voice was that quiet inner voice I've come to identify as the Holy Spirit.

It is part of my daily devotional practice to read from the Scriptures. Over and over again I've found that when I hit the wall, a verse that previously didn't mean anything or make me feel anything in particular is somehow brought back to me and illuminated in a way that feels undeniably clear, personal, and direct. And that day, I felt the nudge to go back and reread a psalm that lodged in my memory: "For you girded me with strength for the battle; you made my assailants sink under me" (Ps. 18:39, NRSV).

I know that Jews and Christians have recited and sung that line millions of times in prayer and worship around the world, but in that moment it lit up as if it were written in the stars for me like a personal letter from God. It became my mantra. "You have equipped me with strength for the battle." I wrote that phrase on sticky notes and stuck them on my computer monitor, my truck's dashboard, and the bathroom mirror. Several times on Sunday, as the people were singing, I would recite that verse: "You have equipped me with strength for the battle." With my eyes closed, I would feel the very strength of the Lord fill my heart through these words!

Looking back at that time, I realize that I wasn't just remembering the verse; I was rehearsing it. I adopted it as my new narrative. I made it *my* story. Maybe I was weary. Maybe I was depleted. Maybe I wasn't strong enough in my own strength. But God was giving me strength. A new strength was being proclaimed over me and into me; God's strength was becoming my own. Having this verse as a clear word from God didn't mean I was also given a five-year plan, a GPS, or even clear directions for what to do in the next moment. There were still plenty of things I did not know about the road ahead. But here's what I did know for sure: *God was with me in the battle*, and that would be enough.

Joshua and Me

The ancient Book of Joshua was written about a particular place and people, yet it is also very much a story about every place and every people. It is a story about transition, a story about moving out of the in-between and into the place where you've never been. There are particular battle stories to be told. And yet in some ways Joshua tells all our battle stories.[1]

The biblical story of Joshua, like my story, is a story of a man without the proper experience or credentials for the battle lying ahead. Joshua had the unenviable task of coming after Moses, a man used by God to perform miracles, a man who spoke face to face with God, a man who spent so much time in God's presence that his face was literally aglow with God's glory. How do you lead in place of a person like that?

In this way, Joshua wasn't unlike most of us—he was not specially trained, competent, or qualified. He was just the guy God chose to lead the people of Israel into the land—not because of merit, experience, or the strength of his résumé but because God chose him and filled him with the strength necessary to lead. Joshua was not a man with an exceptional pedigree. He was a man who believed God would give him the strength to lead the people into a new land of blessing.

On Not Working Harder (but Believing and Trusting More!)

To enter the new normal God has for us, we must defeat enemies, conquer territories, and lean in to our stories. Like Joshua, we are staring eyeball to eyeball with giants that currently occupy that land. To defeat them will require more than willpower and hard work. It will require that we experience a strength we do not possess on our own.

This book is not the kind that says if you grit your teeth, try harder, and put in more hours, you will have the life of your dreams. That is not how spiritual life works at all! It is so much more about God's work in and through us than about our efforts; it's about us yielding and surrendering rather than making it happen.

> To enter the new normal God has for us, we must defeat enemies, conquer territories, and lean in to our stories.

In short, I don't want you to try to work more for God! But I do want you to develop the discipline of focused, consistent trust. Early on in the Book of Joshua it is very clear that whether the battles were going to be won or lost was up to God, not Joshua. Any victory would come from God's strength, not his. The battle would be won or lost based on whether Joshua and the people of God would take God at His word. In the words of Joshua 1:9, "Have I not commanded you? Be strong and courageous. Do not be afraid; do not be discouraged, for the LORD your God will be with you wherever you go" (NIV).

The journey will be demanding, to be sure. The land will seem to demand its pound of flesh. Entering the promised land will not be easy—a new normal never is. The best part of walking into a new season in your life is that it doesn't depend on your strength or your ability because we know that God is the One who gives us the strength and with it the land. God told Joshua three times in Joshua 1 alone to be strong and courageous because He would be with him wherever he went.

God did not say that you would always know where you are going but that the Lord would go with you wherever you go. God did not say that there would be nothing to be afraid of but rather that you don't have to be afraid or dismayed. The voice you hear in your head, the voice you hear when you look in the mirror might be loud and even bullying. But the still, small voice tells you another story; it calls you to believe a different account. Whose report will you believe?

Ultimately, whether you will move into this new land doesn't have anything to do with what you believe about *you*. It has everything in the world to do with what you believe about the One who has called you—what you believe about God. Out in the wild, strength training doesn't have anything to do with obstacle courses, impossible tests of brawn, or being willing to put in more hours or more effort. On the precipice of the land, strength training has to do with believing.

The Power of Belief Changes Everything

Coming into the new normal God has for you has nothing to do with being the fastest, the smartest, the most attractive, or even the bravest. The kind of strength God calls for *always* begins and ends with taking God at His word. That's what biblical strength is all about: believing what God says more than what anybody else says and even more than what we say about ourselves. We must return to this principle over and over again. The strength that God is calling for isn't to have more willpower or to never break a sweat. It looks like trust. God speaks, and we take God at His word and act on what He says.

Men and women throughout history have embodied this kind of strength. They chose to live life outside of the safe zone, wading into the deep end of faith, entrusting themselves to God in ways that looked like utter nonsense to anyone watching. George Müller is a prime example of that kind of trust. Known to gamble, drink, and steal as a teenager, Müller found himself locked in prison for nonpayment of hotel bills at sixteen years old. Four years later, God radically transformed his life and set him on a path marked by extraordinary faith.

Time and again, Müller faced insurmountable odds in following God's call. His legacy is nothing short of astounding, but his story's distinctive factor is the strength of his resolve to believe and trust God. Throughout the nineteenth century he preached in forty-two different countries, traveling more than two hundred thousand miles, addressing over three million people, and leading hundreds of thousands to Christ—all while caring for more than ten thousand orphan children.[2]

The narrative of his life repeatedly evidenced bullish confidence in God's power to work on his behalf. On one trip, he found himself stranded off the banks of Newfoundland. The fog was so dense that the *SS Sardinian*, the steamer he was aboard, had come to a complete standstill. To most people this situation would seem impossible, but Müller was a man who looked at life through the lens of trusting God no matter what.

> **Coming into the kind of life God has for you has nothing to do with being the fastest, the smartest, the most attractive, or even the bravest. The kind of strength God calls for *always* begins and ends with taking God at His word.**

On Wednesday, with no sign that the fog would lift, Müller approached the captain and informed him that they must reach Quebec by Saturday afternoon. The captain blew off the request as impossible, saying the weather was simply too dangerous for sailing. Without any hesitation Müller responded, "Very well, if your ship can't take me, God will find other means to take me. I have never broken an engagement in fifty-seven years."[3]

Bewildered, the captain replied, "I would willingly help you. How can I? I am helpless!"[4]

Instead of giving up, Müller introduced the captain to a new way of navigating life when he simply said, "Let us go down to the chart room and pray." The captain would later report that he wondered what lunatic asylum this man could have come from.[5]

Müller, looking through the lens of trust, said, "My eye is not on the density of the fog, but on the living God, who controls every circumstance of my life." He then knelt and prayed a simple prayer for the fog to be lifted in five minutes. The captain was filled with awe by what he was watching. When Müller finished his prayer, he turned to the captain and said, "Captain, I have known my Lord for fifty-seven years, and there has never been a single day that I have failed to gain an audience with the King. Get up, Captain, and open the door, and you will find that the fog is gone."[6]

At that moment, they opened the door, and the fog was gone. "On Saturday afternoon," the captain later reported, "George Müller was there on time."[7]

This amazing event illustrates that in God's economy, *strength* is just another word for *trust*, a way of standing on the promises and goodness of God. Müller's story lives on—not because he was the perfect Christian but for one reason: he believed God, and miracles happened.

> **Remember this: the resistance is always the greatest when you are on the precipice of significant life change.**

Does that tell you how much believing and trusting God—standing by faith on His promises—matters in the grand scheme of your life? Do you have the strength, the courage, the audacity to take God at His word?

You don't have to figure anything else out. The first step on a journey of faith—toward walking into your new normal, into the land of promise God has for you—is always a simple step of believing.

It doesn't matter where you come from. God isn't asking you questions about your family lineage or investigating your past mistakes to decide if He will use you. Remember Müller's life. Before God called him, he was in prison. It doesn't matter what you've done in the past. What matters is what you do with this moment right here. You get to start now. You have an opportunity in this moment. God is asking the question "Are you willing to trust Me here, now, today?" No muscles, intelligence, or moralistic perfection is required. The only question is whether you are going to believe God.

Remember this: the resistance is always the greatest when you are on the precipice of significant life change. But take the step anyway because believing God *changes* everything!

MORE HEART

Be strong and courageous, because you will lead these people to inherit the land I swore to their ancestors to give them.

JOSHUA 1:6 | NIV

MORE IS A problematic word for many because we tend to want more of the wrong things, or we find ourselves feeling that God wants more or demands more of us than is required. The pursuit of more for more's sake—more money, influence, square footage, or social media followers—is not the currency of the kingdom of God. You don't need more of those things to fulfill God's purposes for you in the world. And gratefully, God doesn't require more than whatever He has already placed in your hands; you don't need more resources, more stamina, more power, more ideas, more friends, or even more knowledge to do what you are called to do.

Our English word *courage* comes from an Anglo-French word that means more heart. A courageous person, then, is a person who is distinguished by having more heart. He is wholehearted in what he's doing. He is all there, and he is all dialed in. He may not be perfect, but he has integrity. He is "integrated"—all of him is moving in the same direction.

If you want more courage, in reality what you need is more heart. That doesn't mean that your knees won't ever knock or that your heart won't ever flutter. More heart doesn't mean you never feel uncertain, intimidated, or outmatched. More heart doesn't mean you naturally live in perpetual tranquility, or that you are always calm and collected. More heart has to do with courage. If strength, as we learned in chapter 1, is related to trust in God, courage is what happens when God's strength permeates your soul. Living with *more* heart has to do with the resolve and focus that flows from a *convinced* heart.

"We are more than conquerors through him who loved

us," the apostle Paul said in Romans 8:37. The idea is not that we'd meagerly survive, that we'd barely get by, or even that we'd merely win, succeed, or conquer. Rather it is that we are *more* than conquerors. There is a kind of victory that God makes possible that transcends our feeble ideas of victory.

High Stakes at the Steak 'n Shake

The breakfast turned out to be fateful, but hardly fancy. We were eating biscuits and gravy at the Steak 'n Shake when my friend tried to talk me into moving from Kansas City to pastor James River Church in Springfield. I heard him out because I was genuinely trying to be open to whatever God might want to do. But deep down I just wasn't feeling it. I sat down at the table, sure that I didn't have what it takes to lead a fledgling church. I had already planted a church and found the whole process of digging out a faith community from the ground up to be emotionally and spiritually exhausting. The journey had been hard—and more than thinking about transitioning *in* ministry, I was quietly considering transitioning *out* of ministry.

> **If strength is related to trust in God, courage is what happens when God's strength permeates your soul.**

So after hearing him out, I told him calmly, "Let me shoot straight with you. I think this church has a lot of promise, but I just don't think I'm your guy." This turndown was supposed to end the conversation. You tell somebody you're not the guy, and you expect them to understand—and then ask for the check.

But instead, he did something extraordinary and unexpected. He looked back at me, eyeball to eyeball, and said, "Well, I don't agree with you. I think you are the right guy, and I hope you'll come." His response startled me. And just like that, something inside me shifted. I went from resignation to possibility in one sentence. I was trying to politely say, "I can't," and he looked back and told me, "You can."

And that one moment, without exaggeration, changed my life forever. I think back over my life, to the thousands and thousands of people whose lives have been somehow changed through the ministry of James River Church over the years. We've seen God show up and do things that defied our wildest dreams, and still do. I didn't have the vision for any of it, didn't have the heart for any of it. I was exhausted. I was discouraged. But one man's words over breakfast ignited a fire in me, awakened a kind of faith in me that I didn't know I had. In that moment, I caught a glimpse of the truth that God wasn't done and my calling hadn't changed.

The words of a friend caused me to see what might be through the eyes of faith, and that got ahold of me. I didn't believe in myself, but he believed in me, and he believed in God's calling and hand upon me. And that was enough. He was speaking to one guy over biscuits and gravy, but ultimately, he spoke to something so much bigger: the destiny of a people, of a church. He wasn't speaking into just my calling but the calling of people I had not even met yet.

That is how it is when God speaks—it is never just *for you or about you*. The call to occupy the land, to enter a new normal, isn't a call to try to realize your hopes and dreams to be rich and famous or whatever. When God calls you to be courageous, it is not just for you; it always affects the people around you, even people you have not yet met.

I often think back to that fateful breakfast conversation I had at Steak 'n Shake. It reminds me that one man's words of courage spoken over me and into me changed the trajectory of not only my life but thousands of others! He chose to speak possibility when all I could see was impossibility, to speak faith when I felt faithless. Such is the power of our words to alter the shape of things and empower not only us but also the people around us to inhabit the land God has called us to!

The Stakes of Your Call to Enter the Land

Over and over again—first to Moses and then to Joshua—God says to be strong and courageous. And to the average person this might seem like some kind of personal mantra or motivation to be your best you, stick to your diet, excel at your job, or achieve some kind of personal life goal. But the stakes are so much higher than that. In Joshua 1:6, God says, "Be strong and courageous, *for you shall cause this people to inherit the land that I swore to their fathers*" (emphasis added). The reason you are called to be strong and courageous is not for you or about you; it has direct implications for everyone around you.

God called Joshua to be strong and courageous so that "this people" would inherit the land promised to them. *This* people. You are not called to an abstract people but a particular people, in a particular place, in a particular time, promised a particular land. God calls you to be strong for the people right in front of you—*your* people!

God did not create us as tiny, self-contained islands, with each of us only responsible for our individual destinies and personal dreams. No, God has designed us to be contingent, dependent—not just on God but on one another. Our stories are bound up together in God. A life of sin is ultimately just a life consumed with self. To live for and to ourselves is to choose death. To embrace the new normal that God has for us is to recognize that it will directly impact the lives of the people around us. The fulfillment of God's promises in our personal lives will undoubtedly cascade into the lives of those we are in relationship with. And the converse is also true—a lack of courage will also cascade.

> **When God calls you to be courageous, it is not just for you; it always affects the people around you, even people you have not yet met.**

If Joshua had not heeded God's command to be strong and courageous, the people around him would not have inherited the land. That's a sobering thought, but a necessary one—that whether the people around us will be able to live in all that God has for them *is* somewhat up to us. We do carry the weight of helping the people around us see the promises of God fulfilled in their lives. If I'm not strong and courageous as a husband, it will affect my wife, Debbie. If I'm not strong and courageous as a father, it will affect my children. If I'm not strong and courageous as a grandfather, it's going to affect my grandkids. If I'm not strong and courageous as a pastor, it will affect the people I am leading.

The call to a new normal always requires more heart, but the good news is that when God gives a command, it's always accompanied by a promise. If you do this, God says you'll "have good success wherever you go" (Josh. 1:7). If we are willing to trust God in this way, the payoff is massive. To live with more heart is to live in such a way as to have success "wherever." Yes, our lives are connected—we need one another, and we come into the promised land as a people; nobody occupies new land alone. But success is not contingent on being in the right place at the right time or reading some kind of cosmic tea leaves to make sure every moment is somehow on script.

God doesn't tell Joshua exactly *what to do*; He just tells him *how to be*. He says, "Be courageous, because I'm with you wherever you go." We don't have to understand some scripted plan and make every decision in perfect accordance with it. He says "wherever." There is no border or boundary to the command, geographically or otherwise; it extends to wherever we are. So maybe you have not been in this place or this situation before. Take heart; it isn't about your experience. It's not even your strength but God's strength, ready for you to appropriate.

It is interesting to consider that even with all the things God does for us, we are still the ones commanded to be strong and courageous. If Joshua is to lead Israel into a new normal in the Promised Land, he will have to choose to take on this courage and pick it up. If the people around him are going to experience the blessing of God, *he* will have to be strong and courageous. The same is true for you.

Moms and dads, single parents, if your kids are going to know God's blessing, you don't have a choice. And this word isn't just for parents; wherever you find yourself, God has new things He wants to do in and through you that will bless the people around you, but they will require more heart. You have to be strong and courageous.

> **God doesn't tell Joshua exactly *what to do*; He just tells him *how to be*.**

What God asks from us is not a feeling we can conjure—of course, we don't always *feel* strong and courageous! But this is deeper than an emotional reality. It is a choice. It is about resolve. It is about our inner constitution, our disposition. It is not a call to denial. There *are* giants in the land. Ancient Israel was going to have to take on seven nations more powerful than themselves. God does not ask us to bury our heads in the sand, pretend that the challenges are not legion, or that we have more money in the bank than we do, or that the road is somehow going to be easier than it appears. No; we are realistic about the fierceness of the opposition within and without. We are fully aware of our limitations. But we are commanded to choose to be strong, to choose courage, trust, and bravery. We choose to move forward in trust, even though we know the outcome is not guaranteed.

When my friend spoke faith into me over breakfast at the Steak 'n Shake, it created a possibility where there was no possibility. But it also created a choice: what to do with the moment I was given was entirely up to me. I still had to *choose* whether to come to James River! I still had to take a step of faith. At the time, I didn't have a burning heart for Springfield, Missouri; I didn't have any sort of blazing "vision." Having walked through months of discouragement, I didn't have a heart for much of anything before I came to James River, but that's how making a spiritual commitment works. We take a step of faith and conviction, and then courage, strength, and vision come to us. Grace comes to us, but the step comes first. The choice comes first.

I want to encourage you not to internalize this as some weight but to hear this as an invitation to holy responsibility. Even as you read this, I believe the Lord is speaking to your heart. He is prompting you to believe Him for more. At the very least He is challenging you to consider that your life could be very different. But remember, the stakes of what you do with what you've heard are not just *your* stakes; your act of stepping into the land you are called to occupy is crucial for the people around you to step into the land they have been called to occupy.

To Be Courageous Is to Be a Person of Conviction

Courage is a strong word. It is good and right to be courageous in all kinds of ways and all kinds of directions. But we also don't have the bandwidth to put our whole heart everywhere. As courage fills our hearts, we find ourselves doing life with a focused resolve, a conviction. Convictions guide and tether our lives; without them we are aimless. Convictions aren't preferences. Preferences live at the surface. Convictions live at the core. There are plenty of things in life I have preferences about, but that makes no difference at all as to whether I live a powerful life. A powerful life is lived from conviction, not preference.

It's important to differentiate between convictions and preferences so that you prioritize your convictions. While your list of preferences may be endless, you will find that your genuine convictions are much fewer in number. Of course, some Christians try to make all their religious preferences into convictions, which always leads to disaster, creating legalism and judgment. Not everything you believe about God or life with God needs the weight of conviction! It's better to keep your list of convictions lean, which will prioritize what's important in life.

I have already been less than subtle in my claim that belief is central to absolutely everything; it is the key to everything. Thus in my life, prayer and reading/studying Scripture have been the two convictions I hold to be most central, precisely because these are the practices that build my faith and allow me to exercise trust, even when I don't feel courageous. Whenever I have had the opportunity to take new territory, it has required me to lean more heavily on my time with God in prayer and His Word—not because I'm trying to earn God's favor or acceptance but because these practices empower courage.

I have strong convictions about prayer because I am genuinely convinced that prayer makes *the* difference between what we see and don't see in life. It may sound stark, but in my experience it is this simple: people who pray receive from God, and people who don't pray don't. In words from James 4:2, "You do not have, because you do not ask." For a Christian, prayer is a practice as vital as breathing. Prayer is our most central and crucial connection, a way of being in the world with God. It is not about legalism, human effort, or work. Prayer puts us in a posture of receiving. It is a way of opening our hearts and hands to all that God has for us.

I believe God wants to bless every person and every church. While God is good to all His creation, there are some things God will not do in us, through us, and for us unless we open our hands and get into this posture of receiving.

Life revolves around our convictions. We make time for what is important, prioritizing what matters. If something is a conviction in your life, it does more than make the list; it grabs your heart, directs your energy, and finds expansion in the daily events of your life.

> **I am genuinely convinced that prayer makes *the* difference between what we see and don't see in life. In my experience, it is this simple: people who pray receive from God, and people who don't pray don't.**

It could also be said that convictions don't flex, while preferences do. We can and should bend our preferences easily and often, based on people's needs and responses. Our preferences should be malleable. Our convictions cannot be. When we are convinced or convicted, nothing is up for negotiation.

Being a person of conviction matters, especially in a world where so many are content to let the winds of culture dictate their passion and perspective. When we act according to our convictions, it develops an even deeper resolve. Acting out of our convictions creates a kind of energy, momentum, and power that keeps us moving forward, giving us the courage to walk on even when the river in front of us feels uncrossable. We cannot be wholehearted if we don't set our intention in a particular way. But when we do set our intention—when we establish our convictions—convictions give us courage.

PRACTICE

Have you settled on your convictions? What are your core convictions? What convictions guide your family's priorities? There is something powerful about articulating where you stand. If you have never given thought to your convictions, I want to encourage you to stop right now and write them down. This is important because having courage without clear convictions is almost impossible.

You don't need many convictions; being convinced about too many things is the path toward being stubborn and obstinate! But to be convicted about a few things— a handful of things of which you are truly convinced— creates a spiritual power and dynamism in your life that propels you forward. *Convictions create courage.*

From convictions, you and I make courageous *spiritual*

commitments that set the stage for the new normal. What would it look like to act in faith regarding the handful of things you are already convinced of? One spiritual commitment gives you the courage to make the next commitment, and the next, and the next. From a mere handful of seemingly small spiritual commitments the trajectory is set for a life of faith and faithfulness.

But it all begins with you making a choice. God gives you strength, but as always, God is relentlessly committed to preserving your free will. You get to choose whether to act on what you've heard. What are the spiritual commitments that you can choose to make today? Choose to have a heart for God now. Choose not to live in fear—even if you still feel it in your bones somewhere. Choose to be strong. Choose to be courageous. And God will go with you.

Speak With Courage

The Bible says, "Death and life are in the power of the tongue" (Prov. 18:21). At that Steak 'n Shake breakfast my friend spoke words of life that gave me courage. His words resulted in the courage that led me to a new normal. The words we speak to ourselves about ourselves and the words we speak to others can bring courage or they can discourage. Joshua was successful in conquering new territory because he spoke words of courage. As he prepared the Israelites to cross a flooded Jordan River, he said, "Consecrate yourselves, for tomorrow the LORD will do wonders among you" (Josh. 3:5). Over and over again Joshua would display courage by speaking courageous words. Without those spoken words a new normal would have been impossible.

There's a reason God spends so much time speaking

words of hope into us, reminding us of His faithfulness. It's because no matter how vast or intimidating the land in front of us might be, we've all been here before, even if we haven't specifically been *here*. We have already been in situations where we just knew there was no escape, yet somehow God made a way. God speaks words that stir up our holy memory and call us back to the miracles He has already done.

> **From a mere handful of seemingly small spiritual commitments the trajectory is set for a life of faith and faithfulness.**

The way we talk matters. Words spoken in faith and hope will empower, embolden, and build bridges into the good future that God has for us. Conversely, if we speak negativity, discouragement, or despair, our words can be as much a force of chaos, unbelief, and disorientation as they could be for good.

And yet surely at least part of what Joshua has to say to us is that how we approach these very real lands has a lot to do with our rhetoric. Whether we will enter the promised land has much to do with how we speak about it and even how we speak about ourselves. I know—this might seem mushy, ooey-gooey, or New Age if you are cynical enough. But I'm not talking about New Age; I'm talking about a *new normal*. Our words do more than articulate our fluctuating, often arbitrary feelings that come and go. They inevitably shape our destiny in a very real way, whether we intend them to or not. Especially when our internal voice of criticism is loudest—the words of accusation, self-loathing, self-doubt, and condemnation can be deafening. When we listen to this kind of critical self-talk—and all the more when we repeat these self-defeating things—we deplete our strength!

PRACTICE

What words do you say *about* yourself *to* yourself? That is the question. We will inevitably feel a roller coaster of feelings—feelings come and go, rise and fall, with or without our consent. We don't have full autonomy over everything that we *feel*.

But unfortunately a lot of us have thought that being true to ourselves means being true to these very fleeting, very transient feelings when nothing could be further from the truth! We are not what we *feel*. We are not called to be true to our temporal feelings but to our *convictions*. In fact, our convictions can be at odds with our feelings, so we have to speak out of our convictions. Our feelings are often not chosen; our words always are.

I remember hearing German evangelist Reinhard Bonnke, who passed away during this book's writing, preach about Peter walking on water. I'll paraphrase what I remember him saying: "Peter didn't walk on water. You can go to any body of water right now, and you'll find that water won't hold you up. When Jesus called Peter to walk on the water, Peter walked on the *word*. Peter walked on the C-O-M-E." The point is simple but profound: the water didn't hold Peter up but rather his faith in what God had said. We are constantly confronted with a similar decision. Will we stand on the shifting tides and endless waves that are our feelings? Or will we stand on the steady, unchanging Word of God by speaking its truth over our lives?

It is not trusting in something we can do but rather trusting something that is being done to us and through us. The further we go, the more consistently we see how science backs this up. Even those outside Christianity acknowledge the power of self-talk, the power of faith. It is not something for us to do but something for us to believe! God does God's part, which is all the heavy lifting—then we have to do our part, which is only to believe what God has already said about us.

> **Whether we will enter the promised land has much to do with how we speak about it and even how we speak about ourselves.**

Yes, the torrent of negative self-talk will come like the waves to tell you that you are not strong enough, smart enough, influential enough, or pretty enough. It will tempt you to compare yourself to someone else. Those feelings may be real, but they do not define who you are or the borders of God's calling on your life.

As it was when I heard the voice of the man in the mirror, there is always a surer, steadier voice calling out to you. That voice doesn't speak of the way things *feel* now but of the way things *are* now. It's the voice of truth from the One who is truth. That is the voice that gives you strength. It is the voice that gives you the power not to fixate on whatever is happening inside yourself but to think of something outside yourself.

> **Our feelings are often not chosen; our words always are.**

I don't know who has labeled you, named you, spoken against you, or spoken into you. But I know that a better word has been spoken over you than the words spoken out of fear. It is the voice of the One who calls you beloved. It is the voice that says in the words of 1 Peter 2:9, "But you are a chosen people, a royal priesthood, a holy nation, God's special possession, that you may declare the praises of him who called you out of darkness into his wonderful light" (NIV). You are chosen, royal, special, and summoned by God out of the ordinary into the new normal. God's voice calls you into the land even now; He tells you that you are not defeated or unqualified. Rather, you are more than a conqueror. His voice calls you to take the promised land.

This call is not merely to believe the best about yourself but to believe what God has said about you. It's a call to let His words fill your heart, renew your mind, and become part of how you see yourself. Words of courage would prove invaluable for the people of Israel as they entered new territory.

> Joshua said to the people of Israel, "Come here and listen to the words of the LORD your God....Here is how you shall know that the living God is among you and that he will without fail drive out from before you the Canaanites, the Hittites, the Hivites, the Perizzites, the Girgashites, the Amorites, and the Jebusites."
> —JOSHUA 3:9–10

Standing on the banks of the Jordan River, the people needed to hear words of courage. They needed someone who would dare to speak the courage and hope of God over them and into them. Just as I needed my friend at Steak 'n Shake to speak into my life that day, we all need a faithful community to speak God's word over us and into us, to see God's hand and calling on us when we cannot see it for ourselves. I would have missed out, and so many people who are important to me now would have missed out on so much if my friend would not have spoken a word of spiritual challenge over me. The story of a person's entire life can take on a different trajectory because one person chooses to speak with spiritual courage in their conversations!

> **It is not trusting in something we can do but rather trusting something that is being done to us and through us.**

This is one reason church is so important. It's one of the reasons Hebrews 10:25 tells us not to neglect meeting together. I know many people today question whether having a relationship with a church is important so long as they have a "personal relationship with God." Still, I contend that having a concrete connection with a local body of believers has never been more important. It's why during the COVID-19 pandemic we went to great lengths to keep people at James River connected online. Because we believe it when God says it is not good for us to be alone, and that God designed us to need one another in this way. We need to live our lives close enough to hear words of encouragement, and sometimes even words of warning, from other believers who can see both gifts and blind spots that are largely hidden from our view. There is a reason Paul calls the church "the body of Christ"—we are designed to depend on one another in this way!

> **There is always a surer, steadier voice calling out to you. That voice doesn't speak of the way things *feel* now but of the way things *are* now.**

"The mass of men lead lives of quiet desperation," wrote Henry David Thoreau in 1854.[1] The same is true today. You never know what kind of pain the people around you are in—from the person who runs the checkout counter at the grocery store, to the person we encounter at the gas station, to the server at the restaurant. Everybody has their battles to face. But if you choose to live in God's strength and choose to speak courageous words of faith and hope, God can use you to give somebody else some strength and heart to fight another battle and maybe even enter a new normal. I know, because I can still remember the biscuits and gravy.

03

SETTING YOURSELF UP
FOR A MIRACLE

Joshua told the people, "Consecrate yourselves, for tomorrow the LORD will do amazing things among you."

JOSHUA 3:5 | NIV

WHAT IS LIFE if not a constant series of transitions? We are never sitting still. Sometimes choices made can lead to pain and loss. But for Christians, as we walk close to God, the best is yet to come. We are always going from where we are now into some new land, some promised land, some new season of blessing, "from glory to glory" (2 Cor. 3:18, NKJV). There is never a place of arrival, never a place where we have seen it all, have done it all, or know it all. There is no mythological "there." To follow the God of Exodus is to follow the God who is always—in all times and places—on the move. In Joshua 3 and 4 the key phrase is "cross over" or "pass over." So in Joshua 3:1, they came to the Jordan, and all the people "lodged there before they passed over." The refrain appears repeatedly—*passed, pass, passing*—and it's endlessly relevant for us.

Soon the time will come for you to cross over too. The river is deep, and the river is wide. It stretches in front of you for what feels like forever. Maybe you never imagined you would cross over. But then the morning comes, and with it the opportunity to walk to the other side into the great unknown. More often than not, stepping into the new normal that God has for you will require not only faith but also divine intervention. God has called you to go somewhere that you cannot go without His help. It's going to take nothing less than a miracle.

Of course, you cannot manufacture a miracle. Miracles are part of God's job description, not yours. You can't make the moment happen; you can't force anything. And because God the Father loves to give His children good gifts, you don't have to beg, plead, work anything up, or work everything out. You are not responsible for the miracle making.

But what you can and *must* do is make space for the miracle—you can make yourself ready. You can clear room for God to do what only God can do. That's what *consecration* is all about.

Consecration

Sometimes just thinking about crossing over can be exhausting, but when God is leading the way, crossing over can be exhilarating! There are always new opportunities, new challenges, and yes, new monsters to fight. There are both new blessings and new responsibilities. The life of faith is a life in constant motion, a life on the move.

When we feel the initial exhilaration of forward movement or even just get bored from all the seemingly wasted time of wilderness wandering, it is tempting to charge ahead into the new normal. You might be thinking, "Let's get on with it, then!" And we do indeed have plenty of adventure ahead! The Book of Joshua is chock-full of some of the most exciting stories of adventure in Scripture. And on the heels of all this talk of being strong and courageous, reflexively, we may want to pick up the sword and go charging off into battle!

But before the battle, we need to take a moment to breathe so we can gain the perspective that will only come when we pause. What happens on the battlefield is important—sometimes the battle *is* won on the battlefield. But some of what will happen on the battlefield is determined by what we do *before* we get there. As Eisenhower once said, "Plans are worthless, but planning is everything."[1]

As we saw in the previous chapter, God has already promised to fight our battles for us! If we are walking close to God and He is leading us, we never have anything to fear from the enemy. The fight is won or lost before we get to it, based on whether we make space for God before the battle begins.

That's what this chapter is all about: making space. Joshua 3:5 says, "Then Joshua said to the people, 'Consecrate yourselves, for tomorrow the LORD will do wonders among you.'" At the beginning and end of the day, *wonders* are what we are all looking for, whether we acknowledge it or not. We crave the wonder, that which is somehow other to us, the supernatural—that which transcends nature and goes beyond the boundaries of the world as we've known it.

> **Some of what will happen on the battlefield is determined by what we do *before* we get there.**

People want to believe in the supernatural, no matter what language they use to express it—we see it everywhere in popular culture. And whether or not people chase aliens or ghosts, call astrologists or mediums for direction, search for transcendence through sexual encounters, or try to escape the boundaries of the natural world with mood-altering substances, it's the desire to see the wonders that motivates us all. How many of our movies, television shows, and novels have an element of the supernatural? Even our current fixation with superhero mythology surely speaks to our desire to experience life outside the bounds of nature and gravity and live in a world where miracles are still possible. We want to be amazed and astonished.

I'm convinced that there is a reason for this restlessness. I'm convinced that our God, revealed to us in Christ, is still performing signs and wonders. I believe that blind eyes are still being opened, the oppressed are still being set free, and the dead are still being raised. We are drawn to supernatural horror films and superheroes in spandex because we are restless for miracles on some deep, intuitive level. Somewhere inside us we know we were made for more than the laws of gravity.

Keep in mind that miracles cannot be earned by good behavior, but they can be anticipated by our faith. Everybody wants to see miracles, but not everyone makes space for them. Consecration is what makes all the difference.

Consecration is not about effort; it's about attention. It's about making space for God. Consecration means setting ourselves apart for an intended purpose. At times throughout history, buildings and objects have been set apart for sacred use. The temple and the ark of the covenant were the places where God's presence dwelled in sacred space. Entering those places required consecration. Joshua's call to "sanctify yourselves, for tomorrow the LORD will do wonders among you" (Josh. 3:5, NKJV) points to the fact that we consecrate ourselves today so that we can see God move tomorrow.

A new normal in our lives almost always comes as a result of consecration; a season in God's presence stirs our hearts and awakens us to God's nearness. Joshua gave the people orders to follow behind the ark of the covenant as the priests carried it. The ark represented the presence of God. They were to keep all their focus and attention on the presence, sensitive to every movement, every leading. It meant waiting on the Lord and following the Lord's presence wherever He went—when it made sense and when it didn't.

> **Everybody wants to see miracles, but not everyone makes space for them.**

Many times we have this idea that if God wants something to happen, it will happen. That is not necessarily the case. Sometimes people miss out on what God would have done—perhaps even what He *is* doing—simply because they are unwilling to consecrate themselves. They are too wrapped up in the things of the world (in Paul's language, not the earth itself but the systems of earth that conspire against God and human flourishing). The word *consecrate* in Hebrew is *kadesh*, the same word translated as "holy" in the Book of Isaiah.[2] It describes a radical setting apart for the purposes of God. It involves separating ourselves from anything that would inhibit us from wholeheartedly devoting ourselves to God.

For this reason we have to be cautious about any behavior or habit that numbs us to the presence of God. When we become more aware of God's power and presence, we become more aware of our shortcomings. We become mindful of the things we've allowed to creep into our lives that keep us from being fully awake to God—anything that corrupts our vision or keeps us from seeing God. These could be unhealthy habits or things that are not in and of themselves wrong but just done in excess. If our brains are full of gaming or binge-watching shows—in some cases full of violence and sensuality—we can numb ourselves to the holy. The internet is full of material that objectifies, defiles, and degrades. And while God offers us grace to cover all these things, if we are going to walk into the land God has promised us, we have to make a conscious choice to walk away from those things that entangle us.

Intentional Seasons of Consecration

It has become significant, both in my life and in the life of James River Church, to have established seasons of prayer and fasting. Among Christian spiritual practices, fasting can be especially misunderstood because it can be construed as attempting to prove our devotion to God with the force of sheer human effort. Nothing could be further from the truth! We fast because sometimes our capacity to hear God gets cluttered and we want to remove all the debris that could keep us from hearing and seeing clearly. Fasting is a way of hitting our inner spiritual reset button. It's not unlike when you lose your internet connection and you have to unplug the router and plug it back in. The signal doesn't ever change—God is always speaking! But our capacity to hear and see does get overwhelmed. Sometimes we have to find ways to reset the inner router.

So much of our lives is about deadlines and demanding schedules to make the most of each day. But consecration always requires waiting. We have to take time to wait on God. Before we move into the land of blessing, there have to be moments for watching, looking, and seeing. The people of God "camped" before they "crossed over." They had three days to sit, to consider the impossibility of crossing a flooded river, to dream about the wonders God would work, and to draw closer to God.

In this particular text, they were watching a flood. Day

by day they saw objects floating down the river in front of them—probably big trees and other debris. The Jordan River is not that big, but Israel had camped on its banks in the rainy season with the snow melting off Mount Hermon and the water coming down into the Sea of Galilee. If you visit Israel today, the spring runoff has been tamed, and the Jordan rarely surges. But in Joshua's day the Jordan River would have been a swollen, rushing, angry river of debris. The people knew a crossing needed to take place, but they were acutely aware that it was humanly impossible!

Coming into the new land God has for you often means taking a long and sober look at what lies ahead. Faith is not denial, not a way of simply burying your head in the sand. Faith is being radically honest about what is in front of us. Our words and perspective of faith are shaped not by the somber tone of reality but by the might, strength, and power of the God we are waiting on. God is certainly the God of the real, but He is simultaneously and ultimately the God over the real. With that recognition, faith operates on a frequency above the chatter of the world. It hears differently. It sees differently. It speaks differently. And for the followers of Christ, that makes all the difference.

A couple of years ago a friend of mine named Tom got some very bad news. It's the kind of diagnosis that no one wants to hear. His doctor told him that he had stage 3 lymphoma with a 10 percent chance of survival, even if he had surgery. You would think that news would be devastating to Tom and his family. There was a 90 percent chance his life was over! The doctor advised that it was time to say his goodbyes, plan the funeral, and make sure his affairs were in order. So Tom and his family started to plan, but their planning was different from what most people expected. He began to plan for a miracle.

Tom knew he needed people to pray, so he took every opportunity to ask people to do exactly that. At James River Church we encourage people to write down what they are asking God to do on a prayer card so that others in the church can pray with them. And that's what Tom did—thirty-four times!

As Tom neared the date of his operation, he felt compelled to make sure that he and his family seized the opportunity God was giving them to interact with the specific people they were going to encounter during his hospital stay. He knew this was likely the only time he would ever see or interact with these nurses, doctors, and hospital staff members who would be part of his care. So Tom wanted to do something that he believed God could specifically speak through to every single person he saw.

With that in mind, Tom and his wife went through their Bibles and identified certain verses they believed God would use to encourage particular people. They chose verses such as Job 42:1–2: "Job answered GOD: 'I'm convinced: You can do anything and everything. Nothing and no one can upset your plans'" (MSG). Then Tom and his family printed out the verses and attached each verse to a piece of candy.

On the day I visited him in the hospital in advance of his surgery, I anticipated a solemn environment with a family who would likely be emotional in the face of such a dire situation. What I walked into was almost the complete opposite of what I had expected. The room was a party, and Tom was the host! There was music playing, candy being passed out, and the family was filled with joyful confidence about what God was going to do! Their words were not filled with the grim dread of what the future might hold but with the ways that God's power might invade their hospital stay and work in Tom's body and how the Lord might speak to the medical team caring for him. Tom wasn't unaware of the severity of the circumstances or in denial of the diagnosis, but he also wasn't willing to deny the power of God. And sure enough, after the surgery Tom was completely, miraculously declared cancer-free.

To some people I'm sure Tom's family may have looked a little crazy praying and speaking words of faith when he was virtually given a medical death sentence. But this is precisely why consecration is so crucial—entering the new land of God's best requires us to go places we have not been before and learn to follow the presence of God wherever it leads us, even when it doesn't make sense to us or the people around us.

We have seen miracles come out of our times of consecration at James River. God's direction and provision have always followed those times of quiet consecration. For Joshua the directions that came were, by human standards, bizarre and disorienting. The people of God had spent three days looking at the overflowing river. Now they were given orders to go to a place they had not been and to a path that would take them through a flooding river. They were charged to follow the ark of the covenant as it headed right toward a flooded river. It didn't make any sense. You can't cross a flooded river! You can't—unless God performs a miracle. You can't cross a flooded river unless God does what only He can do to take you into a new normal.

You can imagine how confusing and counterintuitive

this must have been at first. But that is what the three days of quietness prepared them for—to follow the presence wherever the presence led, even when it didn't make sense. And that is what we have to learn to do—follow the presence, wherever the presence may lead us. The presence will lead us to places where we would not choose to go, to be sure. But the presence will also lead us to new miracles and provision we could have never imagined before!

Consecration is the time for us to decide to ask God to come behind us and clean up the mess or trust Him to make the way for us into a new normal. As Bob Goff said, "The way we deal with uncertainty says a lot about whether Jesus is ahead of us leading, or behind us just carrying our stuff."[3] There are so many uncertainties about what is ahead, so much we do not know and cannot know. What will we do about that? Will we allow the uncertainty to push us closer to the presence? Will we get close enough to see where God is leading?

PRACTICE

> How might God be calling you to a time of consecration right now? A practice of setting yourself apart for what God has next for you? Could it be a fast? Have you ever fasted before? What might you fast—what might you give up—to create space to hear the voice of God in your life more clearly? Remember, this is not about punishment; it is about making space. How long might your fast be? How might you use the time, energy, and effort that would normally go into that thing you are temporarily laying down to lean more intentionally into your relationship with God?

Take a few moments to ask God to guide you in this, and then sit for a couple of minutes before responding.

_____

_____

_____

_____

_____

Consecration Sharpens Our Spiritual Vision

Consecration is not empty ceremonial piety or some manic attempt to prove to God that we mean business. That simply has nothing to do with it. Consecration is not for God; consecration is for us! Why do we need times of consecration? Because "you have not passed this way before" (Josh. 3:4). Consecration marks the end of the in-between time and prepares us to move from where we've been to where we need to go now. We need our senses to be clear and sharp, our minds and hearts open. If we are going to step into a new normal, we will need God to perform mighty miracles on our behalf, and that means we have to clear room in our lives and within our very selves for the supernatural work of God's Spirit. Consecration aligns us with the presence of God and the voice of God so our senses are sharper to discern what God is doing and hear what God is saying more clearly. In practical terms, consecration turns our spiritual GPS on so that God can guide us into our new normal!

As we've already seen, wholehearted devotion is

everything. And what is holiness if not wholeness—if not wholeheartedness? That's what John Wesley understood about the life of sanctification, of being set apart: it is nothing more and nothing less than a life of wholehearted devotion. To come into the land, we will need our senses to be sharp, and we will need to attend to God fully. Anything that numbs us to God's voice, goodness, or presence must be set aside—not as punishment but as preparation!

It isn't running *away* from anything but running *into* the fullness of all God has for us. It is about putting aside anything and everything that binds, constrains, or inhibits so that we can be ready for God to move in our lives in extraordinary ways. We are creating space for God!

As we consecrate ourselves, we put aside things that hinder our spiritual vision. Thus we not only prepare space for God to do new miracles in our lives, but as we clear the debris out from in front of us, our vision becomes sharper and more clear to see what God is doing already. I'm convinced that God performs bona fide miracles that we do not see simply because we are not looking for them![4]

When the Moment Comes

The ancient Israelites knew something about crossing the waters. They had heard the story about Moses crossing the Red Sea. To the younger ones it sounded like a legend, like a folktale. After all, it had been a very long time.

Joshua knew he was *no Moses*. He heard the whispers from time to time within the camp; he knew there were plenty of people who would be quick to remind him that he was no Moses! But no matter. He heard the same voice Moses heard. And even though the river was in complete flood stage and the waters sloshed high up against the banks, he knew there was no going back now.

He sent the priests ahead, carrying the ark of the covenant. This act was not empty or ceremonial. The ark represented the presence of God going before them, and if God did not go before them, they had no chance. He watched the priests' feet descend into the mud as they got closer to the water, but their pace was slow, deliberate, and steady. They had prepared themselves for this; they had made their hearts ready, and their bodies followed suit.

God had given Joshua a very particular command for the priests carrying the ark: "When you come to the brink of the waters of the Jordan, you shall stand still in the Jordan" (3:8). As the priests walked in sync with one another, as measured as a bride walking down the aisle, their feet slowly dipped in the edge, feeling the cool, refreshing water between their toes.

They had taken steps of faith, and there was nothing left for them to do. Whatever happened or did not happen now, it was not up to them. Coming into the flooded waters during harvest season, they stopped and simply stood there.

Can you stop for a moment and stand with them? Can you let the truth wash over you that you are not responsible for your deliverance? Can you hear the ancient words of the psalmist in the wind, "Be still, and know that I am God" (Ps. 46:10)? Can you *be still and know*? Can you stop stressing, flailing, striving, running—even stop thinking quite so hard—and just be still?

This is *your life*, but this is *God's moment*. It's time to stop trying to make something happen, and let the miracle happen to you. Making space is what you've been asked to do. It's God's job to perform the miracle.

When the Israelites stopped striving and just stood still, the impossible happened. The waters flowing from above stood still, rising in a single heap on one side. The priests stood still on the now bone-dry ground in the middle of the Jordan River while the entire nation crossed to the other side.

Just as it happened to them, it will happen for you. Prepare your heart and sanctify your mind. But when it is time to walk through the river, stand still—even though people will tell you that you are crazy for just standing there, even though you may fear looking silly, or the stray thought comes: "But what if *nothing* happens?" The miracle comes not for the strongest, the fastest, or those with the most willpower; the miracle comes to those who *stop, stand still, and wait.* It comes to those who are looking.

> This is *your life,* but this is *God's moment.* It's time to stop trying to make something happen, and let the miracle happen to you.

There will still be plenty of ambiguities to navigate on the other side of the Jordan, but one thing is for certain: things will never be the same. Crossing over is a decisive event in Israel's history, and in our own—a moment that takes us decisively from one season into another. In the words of the Old Testament scholar Walter Brueggemann, "The Jordan is the boundary between the precariousness of the wilderness and the confidence of at-home-ness...The Jordan crossing represents the moment of the empowerment of enlandment, the decisive event of being turfed and at home for the first time."[5]

You've been wandering in the wilderness for a very long time, feeling the displacement and disillusionment. It's good to be "turfed"; it's good to have a sense of place, of soil. It's good to belong somewhere, to be connected to the land.

Welcome home. To be sure, there are battles yet to be fought in this new land. But God has also promised us rest and victory here.

04

THANKS FOR THE MEMORIES

In the future when your descendants ask their parents in time to come, "What do these stones mean?" tell them, "Israel crossed the Jordan on dry ground."

JOSHUA 4:21–22 | NIV

N 2001 TOMMY Caldwell, a professional rock climber, was building a platform for his washer and dryer. The concrete floor in his laundry room was cracked and slated, so he needed some shims to level it out. Instead of purchasing them, he decided to make his own. He grabbed some two-by-fours and headed out to his table saw. He placed the two-by-four on the table and began to feed it lengthwise through the saw. The next thing he knew, the two-by-four shot out from the table. Noticeably shaken, he turned off the saw and began to inspect it to see what had happened. There was a dark-colored liquid on the table—where had that come from? He raised his left hand, and his pointer finger was gone. Tommy grabbed the finger, put it on ice, and headed to the hospital. The doctors were able to reattach it, but it was no longer usable. The doctors told him his professional career was over.[1]

Have you ever had something happen that was so earth-shattering you thought you would never make it through? There's nothing like a near-death experience to give your life a new purpose. Maybe your career went down in flames, your marriage imploded, or your future dead-ended, but somehow you made it through. Can you remember making it through something you thought you'd never make it through? Has God ever brought you through something you thought you would never survive? There is nothing like the day after a car accident when every breath feels borrowed and every moment is a sheer gift. Crossing over is no small thing. It takes every ounce of spiritual and emotional energy you have.

So what do you do now? It's tempting to lie down in the middle of this lush green field in the land of Canaan and take a thirty-six-hour nap. You wonder, with as much buildup as there has been toward crossing over, isn't it time now to forget about the past, let bygones be bygones, and just get on with your life? Isn't it time to get on to the next adventure or challenge and fully explore this new land? On the other side of the Jordan, everything feels new—most of all, you. Isn't it time to finally cut the umbilical cord to the past altogether, forget about all this ancient history, and let yourself be someone entirely new? Isn't that what this new land demands of you?

Surely the entire nation of Israel was feeling this swirl of new emotions and ready to move into whatever was next. And yet this is where we see Joshua at his most mature as a leader. Fighting against the pull to slough off the old and get on with the new, he immediately turned everyone's attention to marking the moment. "Select twelve men from the people, one from each tribe, and command them, 'Take twelve stones from here out of the middle of the Jordan, from the place where the priests' feet stood, carry them over with you, and lay them down in the place where you camp tonight'" (Josh. 4:2–3, NRSV). Did you read that? *Tonight.* There was an urgency, an immediacy, a necessity to it. Joshua understood that marking what God has done in the past isn't only about how history will be told but also how the future will be lived.

The Power of Testimony

Tommy Caldwell was told his climbing career was over, and at first, he thought it was too. But not long after his injury, he started training with an intensity he'd never had before. His injury changed the trajectory of his future—not for worse but for better. Tommy realized he could endure and not give up. That mentality charted the course for everything he has accomplished since.

In 2004 and 2005, Caldwell completed the first free ascents (FFA) of several routes of the El Capitan rock formation in Yosemite National Park. He then made the first ascents of some of the United States' hardest sport routes, including *Kryptonite* and *Flex Luthor* at the Fortress of Solitude, Colorado. In January 2015, Caldwell, along with Kevin Jorgeson, completed the first free climb of the Dawn Wall of El Capitan. Their nineteen-day ascent of the Dawn Wall is considered the hardest successful rock climb in history.[2] Tommy's story is an incredible example of something terrible becoming a launchpad for the future.

> **Marking what God has done in the past isn't only about how history will be told but also how the future will be lived.**

Stories—or testimonies—are not limited to sacred spaces. Businesses and other organizations now grasp the benefit of getting people in a room, giving individuals space to share their stories, and absorbing the transformative power this process has on everyone involved. In sharing a trial or struggle that once may have felt lonely, isolating, and alienating, people no longer feel alone. The story of one person's victory—the character of that victory and the hope of it—is also shared by others.

Testimonies alter the entire time line of our stories. They allow us to revisit the past in a way that helps us discern our present and makes a new future possible. If we want to experience the victory of God in our present and future, we have to revisit the work of God in our past.

Nothing about our lives is random or episodic. It's all connected, even when we cannot or do not easily make those connections. Long before we cared about where or how our stories intersected with the story of God's redemptive work in history, God was already writing us into that larger story. God calls us into the good future He has prepared for us, and that good future also redeems our past. God brings continuity, even when all we have experienced is discontinuity.

> **If we want to experience the victory of God in our present and future, we have to revisit the work of God in our past.**

The only qualification for God to make a beautiful story out of our lives is that we trust the storyteller. That means we have to revisit the ways God has met with us before. That means we have to remember. And not only are we called to remember the story but also to rehearse it, recite it, and tell it to ourselves and one another.

This idea is counterintuitive, I know. After all, you are reading this book because you want to move forward into a new future. You want to occupy some new land. And this may be especially hard to hear when you are miles from where you want to be. But here is the thing: the past holds the key to trusting what God wants to do in your future. The memories of how God moved, what God did, and how God made a way for us need to be remembered and rehearsed—and not just the memory of what God has done but also that God is the One who did it.

What's the Story Here?

Our past, present, and future are all different verses of the same song—the song God is making of our lives. Yes, in God the future is always where our very lives are oriented. Christians have been praying for two thousand years, "Your kingdom come, your will be done, on earth as it is in heaven" (Matt. 6:10), and that is a day from the future that God wants to bring crashing into our present. The emphasis, the weight, is always on the future.

Still, you cannot prepare for the future if you don't take the time to review God's faithfulness in the past. I call this sacred memory. As you have already seen, to take the new land God is calling you into, courage is everything! Remembering what God did in the past prepares you for your future and gives you confidence and resolve in the present. You don't need to relocate to the past, but you do need to remember it because the God who met you then and there is the same God who carves out a good future for you. The way to the future is the way of remembering.

Remember, remember, remember. It's so simple, and yet it's the one mental exercise that builds your faith. When the people of God crossed the Jordan River at flood stage onto dry ground, they did not go any farther without stopping to recognize the miracle that God had performed.

> And he said to the people of Israel, "When your children ask their fathers in times to come, 'What do these stones mean?' then you shall let your children know, 'Israel passed over this Jordan on dry ground.' ... so that

all the peoples of the earth may know that the hand of
the Lord is mighty, that you may fear the Lord your
God forever."

—Joshua 4:21–22, 24

Remembering was not the responsibility of the children. Rather it was on the adults to build an altar and to mark the moment in a way that would elicit curiosity from the children. If our children are not curious about what God has done, it's because we have not been faithful to build a monument that would demand their curiosity. It is a curious thing to pile rocks together to mark what God has done, a curious thing that will incite curiosity. When people come later and see these stones, how can they help but ask, "What do these stones mean?" In other words, "What's the story here?"

The past holds the key to trusting what God wants to do in your future.

If we build an altar, they will ask questions. And it will give us a chance, naturally, to tell the story again, to rehearse what God has done for us. "For the Lord your God dried up the waters of the Jordan for you until you passed over" (v. 23). It wasn't just about our great decisions, hard work, creativity, or personal resourcefulness. We are never the heroes of our stories. God was always at work in and through our stories. Remembering what God has done causes you to approach life from a spiritual perspective in a way that prepares you for new victories.

Some of you might get stumped right here because you see a conspicuous difference between the stories of the

Israelites of old and your story right now, namely, you've never seen the seas part. That's an undeniable, irrefutable miracle. Who wouldn't want to mark a miracle like that? Who wouldn't want to build an altar or make a sign? Maybe your miracle stories don't seem nearly so obvious. Maybe your path through the waters didn't seem nearly so neat. Perhaps you feel as if you waded or swam across the river to get from where you were to where you are now.

But here's the fact: regardless of how you got to where you are, you are here now. You made it this far somehow. You are not yet where you want to be or where you think you ought to be, but you are not where you started. You could have drowned in the river or died on the long journey that brought you to the river. But you did not die; you did not drown. You got here someway, somehow. How did you make it this far?

Even if your journey doesn't seem nearly so linear or miraculous, let me suggest that you revisit the story. Rehearse it. How exactly *did* you make it from where you started to where you are now without being completely taken out? How did you manage to survive this far, given the job you lost, the relationship that dissolved, or the addiction that threatened to take you under entirely? I want to make a bold suggestion: the very fact that you are still here, that you made it this far, that you have not drowned yet is evidence enough that somebody other than you has been at work in your story. There was a hand that guided you, led you, held you, and sustained you. Honestly, could you have made it this far by leaning wholly on your own resources?

God made a way—maybe even when you didn't ask Him

to. God brought you out when you saw no way out. God carried you farther than your legs could have ever carried you. Listen to your life a little bit closer. Look at your life a little bit closer. Somewhere there is a story of the goodness and faithfulness of God. There is a reason to find some rocks. There is a reason to build an altar. Maybe you didn't exactly cross the Jordan River, but you crossed over something hard! You made it from somewhere back there to here. Whatever way it happened, it is a story that needs to be remembered and rehearsed.

> **The very fact that you are still here, that you made it this far, that you have not drowned yet is evidence enough that somebody other than you has been at work in your story.**

If you are struggling to find the motivation to move forward into the new normal God is calling you to occupy now, sacred memory is the best place to find it. It's almost a cliché for an actor or actress to ask, "What's my motivation?" As Shakespeare famously noted, "All the world's a stage, and all the men and women merely players."[3] We all have roles in this cosmic drama of redemption, and we are all trying to find our part in the script. (For Christians, the script is the Scripture!) The script is not old, stale, or wooden but lively and interactive, inviting our participation.

There is a way to improvise faithfully, but just as it is in the world of acting, you need to find your motivation. What is driving you? What is carrying you forward? Considering what God has done will give you the energy, grace, and momentum to find your place in the story. Remembering how God has delivered you in the past gives you the motivation and courage to keep going!

Building Our Altars

Throughout my ministry I have sought and listened to the advice of godly men whose years of experience had taught them things I needed to know. As James River Church was preparing to relocate from our original campus to a new property and worship center, I wrote a letter to Dr. Adrian Rogers, who was senior pastor of Bellevue Baptist Church in Memphis, Tennessee, and requested an appointment. For three hours this man who would have been president if he hadn't been a preacher poured into Debbie and me. I still can remember so much of that conversation, it's as if it happened yesterday.

Because we were preparing to move into a new building at a new location, Dr. Rogers spoke to us about the importance of transitions in life and especially transitions in a church's life. He reminded us that helping the church remember its past with thanksgiving would set the table for a new season of blessing. Following our meeting with Dr. Rogers, we spent time identifying the significant things God had done at the church in the past so that we could share them with the people. The services that resulted filled the church with joy and created an atmosphere of expectancy regarding what He would do in the days to come.

To move forward, we had to revisit the past! Remembering what God had done in the past was the path toward what God wanted to do in and through us now. Maybe the concept seems clear to you, but it was revelatory to me.

That doesn't mean we live in the past or become enamored

with past victories. A ship's captain charts his course not by the ship's wake but by the stars. The car windshield is bigger than the rearview mirror for a reason! Where we have been matters, but not nearly as much as where we are going. When God is the One who carves out the path for us, the best is *always* yet to come.

We need to take an inventory of our victories. For the ancient Israelites that inventory meant there was one stone for each of the twelve tribes. A company of millions of people came from those twelve tribes, the product of a covenant God made to bless just one man, Abraham. They had to faithfully remember the victories of the past to make space for victories in their future.

> **When God is the One who carves out the path for us, the best is *always* yet to come.**

If we are to find God in our current circumstances or situation, the best way is to remember what He has done! Those memories stir our faith, renew our vision, and prepare us for the new victories we will experience. We have to remember the story—not to remember so much *how* God delivered us before, because surely the new day will demand a new miracle, but rather to remember that God has always been our Deliverer!

PRACTICE

You don't have to pastor a church to build an altar. God anticipated these conversations would happen in families. He told the Israelites that their children would ask them what the stones meant. Families can build altars to what God has done. Single people can build altars to the faithfulness of God. Friends can come up with ways to remember the goodness of God together. The important thing is that we do something concrete to remind us, something to remember.

Have you ever built an altar? What was a time in your life when God did something worth building an altar for? What is something you could do now to remember what God did in a way that keeps the faithfulness of God constantly in front of you in the days ahead? Stones still work, but you can use anything. You can do this practice on your own, but this one in particular is best done with a group. Even if it's just a few friends or family members, it helps when everyone can remind one another what God has done in us. Take a few moments to reflect prayerfully and remember something good God has done for you. Write an idea or two of how you might creatively build an altar to commemorate that experience.

_____

_____

_____

05

LETTING GO

Then the LORD said to Joshua, "Today I have rolled away the reproach of Egypt from you." So the place has been called Gilgal to this day.

JOSHUA 5:9 | NIV

THERE IS A familiar pattern to change: God nudges us toward the new normal, but upon our arrival we can feel that something is missing. We are excited about the land, but we can find ourselves wondering if we have all we need.

In reality, in the early stages of coming into the new normal, we rarely need to *add* anything, but there is almost always something we hold on to that we need to *subtract*. The routine of life can numb us to the need for change. Besides, familiarity brings with it a comfort like a favorite pair of shoes. We would like a new normal; we just aren't ready until we let go of a few things.

The internal monologue looks like this: Somewhere deep down, you know that the relationship isn't right. But the idea of severing it would be too painful or cause too much chaos in the short term, so you put off the conversation and delay the change, hoping things will somehow work out for the best.

For some, relaxation seems impossible without the buzz of another drink, so you tell yourself that maybe when work is less stressful, the habit of drinking to unwind will change. Or maybe you know deep down that God is nudging you to do something else with your life vocationally. Still, it would hurt too much to sacrifice the extra income right now, so you decide to wait until you know there is absolute financial security on the other side of doing what you believe God is calling you to do. Or you'll try to deal with what you know has become an addiction to pornography when your sexual relationship with your spouse feels easier and more fulfilling.

Spoiler alert: There is never a convenient time to do the

one nagging thing God has been prompting you to do. It will never be easy. That's why you've put it off for a thousand Mondays. There will never be a time when things will be stable enough, steady enough, or calm enough that deciding to cut off an unnecessary attachment is something you feel like doing. Sometimes you just get sick and tired of being sick and tired, and sometimes the voice of God gets louder and louder until you deal with it. Other times the fear that you'll never hear His voice again unless you change prompts the necessary actions. We have to get to a place where, circumstantially, the old way of life just doesn't work for us anymore and we finally decide we've had enough. We can repeat the same old patterns that have held us back on an endless loop, or we can make a painful cut.

> **In the early stages of coming into the new normal, we rarely need to *add* anything, but there is almost always something we hold on to that we need to *subtract*.**

Here's the catch: the provision rarely comes first. Often we are presented with the opportunity to sever something that feels vital to us, not knowing whether God will provide on the other side.

I'm reminded of my friend Joel, who felt for years that God was calling him to vocational ministry. He and his young wife would have dreams about it every week. They felt certain they were supposed to take a ministry position that paid twenty-five dollars a week. But he had a lucrative job, and taking the leap felt ridiculous. Finally, worn down by the constant sense that he wasn't in the right vocation, he gave his two weeks' notice, left his job, and took the ministry position. Within weeks of accepting the role, mysterious checks started coming in whenever the bills were due. He once had a stranger flag him down on the interstate in rural Indiana—he assumed the stranger needed some kind of roadside help with his car—only to tell him that God spoke to him and told him to give him the $250 he had in his wallet. But none of that would have happened unless and until he made the cut.

> **Spoiler alert: There is never a convenient time to do the one nagging thing God has been prompting you to do.**

I've seen it happen in unhealthy dating relationships—people staying in something they know is not God's best with the logic that it's not ideal, but it's OK. "I'll make do until God sends something better along." But that's not how it works.

God rarely sends what you need while you are hanging on to something you know you don't need. If you have an unhealthy habit in your life that you think you can't live without, you can't wait until something better comes along to fill the void—you have to sever the cord first and trust that God will provide on the other side. There's no getting around the risk involved—you don't get to half cut and then wait and see. This cutting away is the hardest step of obedience, but it cannot be skipped.

The Place of Separation

After forty years of wandering in the wilderness, the people of God finally crossed over into the land. The relief in the air was palpable; they could finally feel their feet touch the ground of that fabled land where the milk and honey flowed, where the grass and dirt beneath them felt charged with the promise of God. He had pledged this territory to their ancestors, and now they were finally stepping into it, getting their first taste of the new normal. They knew there would still be battles to fight, but the ground was lush and the future bright. It felt like the good life.

But as they camped at the place called Gilgal, the past caught up with them. God had commanded their ancestors that every male be circumcised, yet none of the men of Joshua's generation had obeyed this command.

> **God rarely sends what you need while you are hanging on to something you know you don't need.**

Circumcision involves the cutting away of the flesh from the tip of the male reproductive organ. God commanded that the circumcision be performed on the eighth day after the child's birth. Think of how much easier it would have been to follow God's original command! It's a fact: delayed obedience often complicates our lives and can result in painful circumstances our obedience would have avoided.

Before the Israelites could enter the land of blessing and keep living in a new normal, they would need to address an area of delayed obedience. In Gilgal what was important to God would have to become most important to them. It was a place of reordering their priorities to align with God's priorities.

If you are going to move into the new normal, this is a crucial question: Is there something God has asked you to do that you have left undone? Is there something that you know God has wanted you to deal with, but you haven't responded to what was spoken to your heart? It could be a besetting sin—an addiction, a habit, or something you call a hobby that in truth has more of a hold on you than you do of it. It could be a relationship that has not been reconciled, and you know you are being led to go back, make an apology, and make amends.

> **It's a fact: delayed obedience often complicates our lives and can result in painful circumstances our obedience would have avoided.**

To the modern mindset a Scripture passage like Joshua chapter 5 might seem like an exercise in divine arbitrariness. What merit could there possibly be in a divine being telling a group of grown men on the heels of crossing into the land of their dreams to stop marching so every male could cut the foreskin off his genitals? It's one thing as a procedure for a baby but a crippling, wrenching experience for grown men who are ostensibly being prepared for battle just around the corner.

As we saw in a previous chapter, God told the people to follow the ark of the covenant right toward the flooding river. God seems to use counterintuitive measures to teach us to trust divine initiatives over our most basic human instincts. But I don't think His choice is arbitrary at all. In

Joshua 5:9 God says, "Today I have rolled away the reproach of Egypt from you." That's why to this day that location is called Gilgal, which means "a rolling away."[1] Gilgal, the place where God dealt with Israel's long-delayed obedience, is also where God dealt with His people's *shame*.

We know more and more now about how shame affects us, not only psychologically but also physically. Shame produces hiding, and secrets kill us. The work of popular authors such as Ed Welch has brought the topic of shame into our public discourse. We are just beginning to understand how shame can affect the body and even be stored in the body through multiple generations. Our bodies do not forget things.

At Gilgal, God forced His people to confront their past and bring the truth of their disobedience into the light. Without this bold and courageous act this generation would be condemned to repeat the same mistakes. In a very public act of obedience the people of God were breaking the cycle of disobedience and shame. They were resetting the entire story. Yes, there would be pain involved in this cutting away. But note that Gilgal was not named as the place of pain but the place where their shame was rolled away!

God is not a monster who delights in watching you suffer. On the contrary God is absolutely, relentlessly committed to seeing you whole, complete, without shame, and not being sabotaged by your past. That's what Gilgal is all about. God will let the past catch up with you—not so you can be conquered by it but so you can confront it and make things right. There's no getting around it: the cutting away of something that has been attached to us can be excruciating at first. We might face a kind of detoxification of spirit, soul, and body that will cause a temporary scream. But that temporal affliction is only for the sake of long-term healing, of making things right, such as when David prays in Psalm 51, "Let the bones that you have broken rejoice" (v. 8). It reminds me of a doctor setting a broken bone, which is painful but necessary for proper healing.

> **God will let the past catch up with you—not so you can be conquered by it but so you can confront it and make things right.**

It could also be said that Gilgal is a place of separation. Sometimes the thing you need to be separated from, the thing you need to sever, is not external but internal. It could be an attitude of pride or self-indulgence. It could be a lingering racial prejudice that you don't want to admit, even to yourself. It could be an old grudge, a slight you have hidden away deep inside and harbored for years that has slowly fermented into bitterness. Some things you have attached to are not things God can bless, and they have no place in the land God is calling you into now. Gilgal is a place of letting go of things you don't need. They are things you weren't meant to carry with you anyway.

If a toxic, abusive relationship in your life is keeping you from experiencing God's best, don't just keep on walking, ignoring the truth you know in your very bones. Gilgal is the place to let go of that man or woman who told you that you could not survive without them, but deep down you know it's not true. You have come too far already to let anyone or anything keep you from being the woman or man you know God has called you to be.

When you are in Gilgal and you are cutting away the thing, relationship, or substance you thought you needed so desperately, it might feel as if you aren't going to make it. But take heart. Gilgal is not the place where you die; it's the place where your *reproach* dies, where your *shame* dies. It's the place where the last remnants of the old life, the unhealthy you, are cut away so you can fully inhabit this new land and journey into your new normal.

The Place of Healing

But there is something else. Gilgal is not just the place for the cutting away—Gilgal is also a place of *healing*. After this cutting away, God didn't ask the people to charge ahead to the next fight—that's how a lot of us got ourselves in this shape to begin with. We charged from one battle to the next without paying attention to unhealed wounds, unhealed trauma, and unhealthy patterns.

> **Take heart. Gilgal is not the place where you die; it's the place where your *reproach* dies, where your *shame* dies.**

God isn't interested in productivity at all costs. That's how God's children worked when they were slaves in Egypt. That's not the new normal; that's not how things work in this new land. God isn't interested in you getting anything done as much as He wants you healed, whole, and rested. Gilgal's message is that it's worth it to stop long enough to take the time to get it right. This is no small message; this is the long, slow, painful work of repentance, forgiveness, and healing. Shame is rolled away, and full restoration occurs. Battles are won and lost. What happens at Gilgal is holy; it's sacred, and it cannot be rushed.

There will be plenty of time for adventure and plenty of time for battle. All too often when we begin to feel pain and discomfort, we want to move on to the next place to do the next thing when the most important work has just begun. Sometimes God's word to us is *"Stay right where you are until you get healed."* Yes, there are enemies in the land. Yes, there is great opportunity. But don't think about that now. Part of what it means to live and thrive in the land is to know when to advance and when to stay still. Displays of toughness are not required but rather displays of obedience that say, "I'm willing to put the rest of my world on pause until God says I'm ready."

This process takes time because the work of healing God wants to do in our lives will require more than a bandage; this is not superficial work. God isn't interested in patching us up to get us back on the field or back on the clock as quickly as possible; He wants to truly make us well. God doesn't want to put a bandage on us but to heal us deeply, thoroughly. The season of rest and healing is what it takes to make us whole instead of merely making us look better.

Yes, there is a time and place for moving on, moving forward, crossing over where you have not dared to cross before. That is good and right. But know it is equally a part of the rhythm of a life with God to take time to stop, to lie down, to sleep, to eat, to recover—to do whatever it takes to get better—and not move until the slow work of healing has run its course in you. This too is obedience.

While this painful act of delayed obedience might have seemed to make the people of God weaker and more vulnerable for the moment, this was the path toward full healing. It was the way God dealt with the shame of their past. What surely looked like an unnecessary, lengthy stop—what would have looked like weakness, vulnerability, and bleeding—was the route to wholeness. The new normal with new victories for Israel required letting go and embracing a very different path of preparation for victory. The same is true for us.

PRACTICE

What is that thing you know you need to cut away? If you are dependent or codependent on someone or something, that is not God. I hate to tell you, but whatever you are afraid it might be—that is probably what it is. You know it precisely because you feel yourself hanging on too tightly—that's why you are so afraid to let go. It is scary to let go of something so attached, something you think you need. It is the most radical and frightening act of trust. It is also the ultimate key to freedom in the land, the most powerful act of release into the new normal.

Whatever or whoever it is, why don't you go ahead and name it right now and hand it over to the One who knows you best and loves you most? And precisely because it is such a big deal for you to relinquish control and let go, why don't you write a short prayer officially telling God that He can have it? It can take whatever form you want but should be some version of saying, "God, I hear Your voice, and I am letting go of _____ to You." Sit with this for a few minutes. It's OK to take your time. It's OK to tell God you're scared to let go, even while you are telling God you are letting go. It's OK to shed some tears. Remember, Gilgal is a place of separation—but it's also a place of healing!

_____

_____

_____

Remembering and Forgetting

For the children of Israel to allow themselves to have this painful surgery and be laid up for days, vulnerable and dependent, was to relinquish control. It was a radical act of trust. But it was not the last way they would be called to relinquish control. Another detail came so quickly that we could easily miss it. Despite all the wilderness' ambiguity and wandering, all the walking in circles, God had been faithful to provide in a very particular way. The manna had been there every morning, just enough for the day ahead—a reliable, dependable provision.

But during this same season of recovery, while the Israelites were camped at Gilgal, they kept the Passover celebration. And on the day after Passover, they ate the produce of Canaan's land for the first time, the unleavened cakes and parched grain. "And the manna ceased the day after they ate of the produce of the land. And there was no longer manna for the people of Israel, but they ate of the fruit of the land of Canaan that year" (Josh. 5:12).

Whoa. That was fast! After all the years that God had

provided manna, they had a season of rest and healing after this circumcision, and suddenly the manna wasn't there anymore. On the positive side, there were new tastes to discover, and the monotony of the old was broken. On the negative side, the reliability and familiarity of the past were broken too.

It is not that remembering the past is by any means bad. As we saw in the last chapter, we need to remember the past. But again, the kind of remembering we are called to is *not* wistfulness or nostalgia. Rather we remember the past because it tells us that the God who called us is working toward our future and for our good. When we remember how God has worked in the past, it's important to remember that our God is always and forever a Deliverer.

One danger of sentimentality and nostalgia is the temptation to long for the old miracle instead of the Miracle Worker. The old miracles, as important as they are to remember, worked in the old land. But the miracle that God used to bring us from where we *started* to where we are *now* won't necessarily be useful to get us from where we are *now* to where God wants to take us *next*. Entering the new normal will require new miracles, which means it will require fresh faith and new leaps of faith. The faithfulness of the Deliverer will always be consistent, but the methodology of the deliverance constantly changes.

> One danger of sentimentality and nostalgia is the temptation to long for the old miracle instead of the Miracle Worker.

So yes, the very day after His people ate the produce from the new land, the supernatural manna God had been providing stopped. Now the people of God were to eat the fruit of the land of Canaan. Being able to partake of the fruit of this new land was a kind of miracle, to be sure, but it was not the same as the manna they simply picked up off the ground to eat. Now they would be required to plant vineyards and till the soil. God would deliver the land into their hands, but there was new work put in their hands to do too. The work would be rich, and the rewards of their labor would be great.

> **We must remember that God always makes a way, but we must not be married to the particular ways God has made before. The old miracles will not sustain us, but the God who performed them absolutely will.**

Even so, it's hard to let go of the old miracles. It's easy to try to rest on the past instead of resting in the Lord. It's tempting to want to cling to yesterday's provision even though on some cellular level we know deep down that what God did for us in the past won't be useful for where God is taking us now.

So the task before us is this: we need to stir up our sacred memory and remember what God did, but not think that's the only way God works. We must remember that God always makes a way, but we must not be married to the particular ways God has made before. As we come into the new normal we are called to, the old miracles will not sustain us, but the God who performed them absolutely will.

06

SEEING WHAT GOD SEES

Now when Joshua was near Jericho, he looked up and saw a man standing in front of him with a drawn sword in his hand. Joshua went up to him and asked, "Are you for us or for our enemies?" "Neither," he replied, "but as commander of the army of the LORD I have now come." Then Joshua fell facedown to the ground in reverence.

JOSHUA 5:13–14 | NIV

OST OF THE time, we only evaluate what's in front of us, what we can see with our physical eyes. In other words, we only see what we can see—and most of the time, we see the world from a natural point of view rather than a spiritual one. But the unseen realities of life are the greater realities. When we are coming into the land God has for us, the task is to learn to see the world and our lives as God sees. Sometimes that happens best when life seems to come entirely off the rails from our limited human perspective.

Not long ago I hit a season in which my life seemed to change overnight. I had been in Rome, leading a tour on the journeys of the apostle Paul. Thankfully, Paul wrote a lot about weakness, because that was all I felt when I went from leading a tour to lying flat on my back on a gurney with a blood clot in my brain. As beautiful as Italy is, all I could think about was getting back home to the world I knew.

> **The unseen realities of life are the greater realities.**

Once we got back to the States, I still wasn't well, so we headed to Colorado, sure that some days in the mountains would bring the healing and rest I needed. On our third day in Vail, I talked Debbie and my daughter, Savannah, into renting some electric bikes to ride along a mountain stream. It was a gorgeous day. As we stopped to take some pictures, Debbie's foot became caught in the bike, and she fell, shattering her pelvis. Her recovery required fourteen days in the hospital. Needless to say it was a difficult time for both of us.

As time passed, instead of getting stronger, I continued to lose weight until I became visibly gaunt. Debbie grew more worried about my health and wondered what was happening. The board of the church wanted to send me to Mayo Clinic, so finally I went. Ultimately they diagnosed me with an autonomic condition that involved excruciating fatigue. Worse yet, there was no cure.

Every year during the summer our church participates in twenty-one days of prayer and fasting. While on the fast that following year, I let the church people know the severity of my situation and asked them to pray for me. I don't know what I expected to feel as they prayed for me, but what I felt most was a deep sense of their love for me. And in the days that followed it became obvious that God had touched my heart physically. Instead of repeated bouts where my heart rate rose to over two hundred beats per minute, it was now calm.

Still, the fatigue was relentless and hadn't diminished. Amid this situation I kept pressing forward on Sunday mornings to preach at the church as best as I could. One Sunday morning about five weeks after that initial touch from God, a couple from the church felt led to anoint me with oil and pray for me. When they did, I felt the fiery presence of the Lord from my head to my feet. Something definitive happened. As I returned to my seat, I turned to Debbie and said, "God just healed me." At the core of my being, I knew God had touched me. Over the next six months I gained forty pounds, and my strength returned.

How did I know God healed me? It was more than

feeling something; there was an inner knowing. As one old preacher put it, "You know that you know that you know." It's spiritual intuition that comes straight from heaven's throne—a moment when we see, hear, know, or understand the supernatural work of God.

What does all of that have to do with you? When everything looks as if it's over from your point of view and you feel as if you have come to a dead end, God calls you to another way of seeing. In God's way of seeing the world, there are no dead ends. What looks like the end to you may only be the beginning of a whole new chapter in this story of God's faithfulness that is being written with your very life. A miracle is not a fluke or a one-time exception. Whenever you see impossibility, God wants to give you eyes to see what is only possible by His great power at work in your life.

This is what it means to follow the God of Joshua, who took His people from the wilderness to the land where milk and honey flow. God was always on the move then. God is still on the move now.

Spiritual Vision

There is another way of seeing the world, another kind of vision—spiritual vision. There are three ways we can cultivate spiritual vision.

1. Spiritual vision comes from being in God's presence.

That's why Joshua could discern and lead with such clarity at every turn—he was a man who prayed. We are regularly confronted with moments where our natural, physical vision and spiritual vision will not easily come into alignment. That's why we must not only stay alert to the presence of God but also spend time in His presence so we can act with discernment when those moments come.

Joshua was gazing at the fortified city of Jericho protected by its storied walls one day when he looked up to see an ominous sight: a large man standing over him with his sword drawn. He seemed to have come out of nowhere. If we reimagine this as a scene out of an old western movie, Joshua, the gunslinger, would be the kind of man who lived with his finger on the trigger. Nobody got the drop on him, nobody snuck up on him, and nobody surprised him until this being did! This angelic visitor was not just any angel—this being was the commander of the Lord's army.

I might have fainted at the sight, but Joshua asked the mysterious stranger a perfectly rational question: "Are you one of us, or one of our adversaries?" (Josh. 5:13, NRSV) It wasn't a bad question, and in a way, maybe it was the only question he could have asked. But it was a very human question—a question based on what he could see with his eyes. Are you on my team or theirs? Are you for me or against me? Are you a friend or a foe?

Because Joshua was a spiritual man, a humble and discerning man who was asking earnest questions and seeking the truth, he was in a position to hear an astonishing answer: "Neither; but as commander of the army of the LORD I have now come" (v. 14, NRSV). And just like that, *snap*! Joshua's perspective completely shifted from a horizontal human perspective to a vertical one, able to see that this was not a mere human encounter but a holy visitation.

To this day scholars disagree as to the exact nature of the mysterious stranger who visited Joshua. Was it an angel? Or was this an appearance of the preincarnate Christ? Was

Joshua the first person to have a conversation with Christ this way? We don't know for certain. But for our purpose, the exact nature of this unusual visitor is not critical.

More pertinent is that Joshua had an alert, clearheaded awareness that came from abiding in the presence of God. He had been praying and waiting on God. He was on high alert. When you pray, you can count on it—whatever needs to be seen, you will see.

But Joshua's interest was not the same as the angelic being's interest. Joshua wanted to know, "Are you for me or against me?" But the stranger had a bigger concern than winning any particular battle that Joshua had in mind. The priority of this incredible being was to serve God and accomplish His purpose.

We often have tunnel vision that zeroes in on whatever particular fight we are in. But when that happens, we can lose sight of the war. We can easily confuse our agenda with God's or assume that our enemies must be God's enemies. The simple truth is that we often see the world from a carnal rather than spiritual perspective, and we lose sight of God's will altogether, which leads to the second way we cultivate spiritual vision.

2. Spiritual vision comes when we submit to God's purpose.

Because Joshua was prayerful and stayed close to the presence of God, his response was not to try to convince the stranger of his plan or argue his case. Instead he discerned the larger purpose of God through the presence of this stranger. Once Joshua discerned that this commander had been sent for a higher purpose, his immediate response was to fall to the ground in worship. He was willing to submit his way of seeing to another way of seeing.

Joshua asked, "What do you command your servant, my lord?" (v. 14, NRSV). He was instantly submissive to the will of God, willing to subordinate his desires, his agenda, and his way of seeing things to whatever God had planned for him. No longer was it about winning or losing; conquering Jericho became secondary to doing God's will. More than personal victory he wanted to honor and worship God, no matter what that meant or what it cost.

A god who simply helps us fulfill our own chosen purpose or desire is no god at all, only an idol. God is not a genie in a lamp or a cosmic Santa who comes to fulfill our wishes. God cannot be tamed or controlled. That's why getting to this point of surrender is everything.

It's not surrendering to a cosmic narcissist who wants to bend us into human pretzels in some attempt to bring him some abstract glory. Part of what's so beautiful about submitting to God is that we are submitting to the One who always has our best interests at heart! There is a tyranny to living in the world's system of winners and losers, insiders and outsiders. What good has playing that game ever done us? What God offers us is not subjugation but liberation. We are free from the game and all the people who play it.

> **Part of what's so beautiful about submitting to God is that we are submitting to the One who always has our best interests at heart!**

It is not that God does not want you to experience victory; it's just that God's victory can take place in peculiar ways. The way God ultimately overcomes the forces of sin and death is through His sacrifice on the cross. God's way of seeing the world is so different that what looks like losing might be winning. But this requires that we completely give up our need to control or have any particular outcome.

Inevitably the path toward the victory God has for us will involve doing things that don't make any sense to us. It's not that God will ask us to do something irrational, per se, but *transrational*—transcending our categories of winning and losing. Sometimes the victory God brings will preserve our lives but not our egos. What if winning in God's eyes requires us to do something that makes us look stupid? We will give up on our attempts to manage our image when we fall to the ground in worship, in complete surrender.

We have to get to a place where we give up our need for personal victory and see ourselves as part of a larger story of God and His purposes in the world. This awareness frees us to be foolish, look silly or absurd, and not take ourselves too seriously. When God asked the Israelites to walk around the city's walls in a kind of parade, showing up at the same time to do the same thing day after day, it was hardly a military strategy! But that is what submission does—it liberates us from needing to make sense. We get out of our headspace and into a "heartspace" of absolute trust, humility, and dependence. Not only do we trust God to win our battles, *but we also trust God to be the One who defines for us what winning looks like*!

When Joshua responded with worship and submission, the commander of the Lord's army told him, "Take off your sandals from your feet, for the place where you are standing is holy" (v. 15). A pattern emerges through the Book of Joshua: the people of God are told to stop and consecrate themselves in some way, mark the moment, and take time to honor God. They do, and victory comes—*after*.

> **Sometimes the victory God brings will preserve our lives but not our egos.**

What does this teach us? To experience victory, we first have to get to a place where worship and obedience matter more than winning.

3. The final way we cultivate spiritual vision is to believe what God says.

Joshua trusted God's promise to deliver the city into his hands. For every single problem you face, there is always a promise. This is not a cliché. God is saying something to you at this moment about the situation you are facing. You may not be able to make sense of it; it may sound outrageous to you.

> **Not only do we trust God to win our battles, but we also trust God to be the One who defines for us what winning looks like!**

That's what happened in Joshua 6:2. God's pledge to deliver the city into Joshua's hands was completely outrageous from a human perspective. But Joshua did the one simple thing that sets heroes of faith apart from the rest: when God spoke to him, he believed. He took God at His word. That was all God ever wanted or required from him— to believe.

There is a wildness to our lives as fragile, created beings, and there are few things we can count on for sure. Precious few formulas for any of it are guaranteed to work. But in the stories of Scripture and our lives we see a pattern where invariably God speaks to the moment.

> **To experience victory, we first have to get to a place where worship and obedience matter more than winning.**

It is more likely to be a whisper than a shout, but the God who created all things is constantly communicating. God will speak some kind of promise to your heart concerning your situation. It can happen in a variety of ways. You might read the Bible and find a verse suddenly leaping off the page into your reality. If you have been in God's presence, you know in your heart when it happens.

When you trust what God says, when you trust God's vision over your vision, God acts. Believing is one thing God cannot do for you; you have to choose to trust. But from there, God will do what only God can do: He will fight your battles for you.

How We See

Our ability to see through the eyes of faith determines the entire trajectory of our lives. According to Proverbs 29:18, "If people can't see what God is doing, they stumble all over themselves" (MSG). A conqueror doesn't need to be the strongest, fastest, or smartest. In everything that matters, all we need in order to win is the ability to *see*. More than anything else, having the vision to see what God sees in any given battle determines whether we will win that battle.

The question is not whether God is doing something. God is always doing something! The question is, *what* is God doing? We need a vision of a deeper reality than what is immediately visible right in front of us. Vision does not determine *what* we see with our eyes; vision determines *how* we see with our eyes.

> **For every single problem you face, there is always a promise.**

Having your eyes open is not the same as having vision. It is possible to have your eyes open and yet not truly *see*. When I'm not wearing glasses, I wear contacts. One time I was preaching at a minister's conference. It was a message I had never preached before, so with the content being relatively unfamiliar, I was somewhat dependent on my notes. While I was in the middle of preaching, I casually wiped my eyes and felt my contacts pop out. In an instant I was flying blind. I couldn't read anything, couldn't see anything. It was a horrible feeling. I had my eyes open, but I could not *see*!

It is one thing to have your eyes open, but it is another thing entirely to see with clarity, to see with perspective— to see with *divine* perspective. To see what we need to see from the right perspective. Too often we cannot see what God is doing because we have become comfortable seeing things from a human perspective.

Think about where our planet sits: inside our galaxy, inside our solar system, inside the universe. Do you realize how fast the earth is spinning on its axis and moving around the sun? We're going more than two million miles per hour, eight hundred miles per second, but from your perspective it looks like we're sitting still. What we see—and how we interpret it—is not necessarily reality. God is doing more than what you can see, so don't live based on your feelings; walk based on your faith instead.

To paraphrase Albert Einstein, the faster you go, the slower time becomes. He theorized that at the speed of light, time stops, and distance shrinks to nothing. Time and space are not constant and universal; they are flexible and personal to the observer. The problem lies not in relativity but in assuming that our common sense represents reality.

> **Believing is one thing God cannot do for you; you have to choose to trust.**

This concept is equally true in matters of spirituality. We come to trust the limited scope of what our eyes can physically see and assume that what we see is the way it is.

Our old way of seeing is especially problematic when we are coming into the new normal. This undiscovered territory to which we are being called is full of new enemies. Having our eyes open will not be enough. It is not merely *whether* we see but *how* we see that will determine *what* we see. The stakes of vision in such a moment are incredibly high—the difference between whether we rise or fall to the challenge before us. To go back to Proverbs 29:18 in the King James Version, "Where there is no vision, the people perish."

Seeing the City

Joshua went from seeing the stranger to seeing the walls of the infamous city of Jericho. As his wide, curious eyes took it in, he saw a city shut up inside and outside, a fortress on the border of Canaan designed to stop invading armies. Even though he was a man of faith, surely he was initially perplexed. The city was fortified, impenetrable. "None went out, and none came in," the Bible says in Joshua 6:1. He was probably wondering how they were going to take the city. He'd never seen a city like it before, never faced a challenge like this one before.

> **Vision does not determine *what* we see with our eyes; vision determines *how* we see with our eyes.**

First Joshua gazed at the city through human eyes, pondering it through his natural understanding. He looked through physical eyes at a physical city, wondering how he was going to seize it. After all, he was a military leader with an army of former slaves, now looking at a fortress perfectly designed to repel any invasion into the land of Canaan. From a physical standpoint the prospect of attacking and taking the city seemed nearly impossible.

This is almost always our experience when we see our new normal through natural eyes. The physical reality of the situation at hand is discouraging, overwhelming, and often even paralyzing. Let's be clear about this: there is a kind of truth—a kind of sober realism—to seeing this way. We see a city that is garrisoned and impenetrable. We know that we physically, humanly, do not possess the ingenuity, strategy, or power to take it. And in this regard, we are not wrong! It is beyond our natural capacity to take the city. We are not strong enough, smart enough, or powerful enough to penetrate the impenetrable. For Joshua to see the city and to be overwhelmed is not wrong from a human point of view; it's reality.

The big caveat here is that this human point of view is not the only reality. There is a different way of seeing. It is the apostle Paul's perspective when he writes in 2 Corinthians 4:18, "We look not to the things that are seen but to the things that are unseen. For the things that are seen are transient, but the things that are unseen are eternal." The human reality of what is seen and temporal is a kind of truth, but it is only a half-truth. Yes, the physical reality is that the walls of Jericho are indeed insurmountable. However, reality is not only physical but *spiritual*! And the spiritual reality is the greater reality. Though we live in a natural world, the truth of the spiritual world runs deeper and truer than our natural eyes can see. The spiritual world is underneath us, all around us, saturating every part of our existence. In this regard, what is spiritual and unseen is even more real and solid than what we read in the newspaper. This spiritual, unseen reality underwrites everything about the world that is visible.

We have to recognize the difference between what we see and what God sees. And in the battle of Jericho there was a difference between what Joshua saw and what God saw. Scripture invites us to a different kind of seeing—a deeper, more intuitive, more Spirit-led kind of seeing. We are not invited to put our heads in the sand and live in denial as if faith were some glib kind of optimism or willingness to see the glass as half full rather than half empty. Rather, like Joshua, we have to behold the city in front of us—to take in the height, depth, scope, and scale of it—and assess it in our human way. To see it and describe it for what it is without some kind of hopeful spin is not faithless, but it is partial and incomplete.

The question is, will you allow what you see with your physical eyes to be *all* that you see? Are you willing to open yourself to a different kind of seeing? Are you willing to trust a different kind of sight and a vision of the world that transcends your natural capacities to see, touch, feel, and hear? Are you willing to trust that there is a deeper mystery at work?

> **Though we live in a natural world, the truth of the spiritual world runs deeper and truer than our natural eyes can see.**

Right after Joshua surveyed the world through his own eyes, he was given a word that invited him to a different kind of perspective—to see the world from a different elevation. Like John's experience in Revelation 4:1, it was an invitation to "Come up here"—to see the same human, physical reality from another perspective. God said, "I have given Jericho into your hand" (Josh. 6:2). That's divine perspective on a situation that, in natural terms, would be completely impossible. That's spiritual vision. It's sharpness and clarity that comes not from optimism but from faith in the living God!

PRACTICE

Pause now for a few moments of prayer, specifically with this question in mind: What struggle or conflict in your life have you only been seeing from a natural or physical point of view that God might want to show you from a spiritual perspective? Ask the Holy Spirit to show you a situation right now that you are only seeing from a human vantage point that God wants to show you from a divine vantage point. Write down any impressions or thoughts that come to you in the silence.

_____

_____

_____

Limitations to Our Vision

Most people experience some degree of challenge with their physical eyesight at some point in their lives. We rightly do not generally have a great deal of stigma or shame around this—it is perfectly normal and human not to see clearly. For that matter, it's completely human not to see perfectly spiritually either. It was, after all, none other than the apostle Paul, surely one of the greatest *seers* and sages ever to walk the earth, who wrote, "For now we see in a mirror dimly" (1 Cor. 13:12). Our vision is not perfect, nor is it expected to be.

That said, the gospel has much to say to us about how we see and the possibility of having our eyes healed to see more clearly. Particularly in John's Gospel a number of physically blind people experience miraculous healing that restores their sight. In a way this sight and blindness run as a deeper metaphor for spiritual life. The restoration of sight becomes an allegory for salvation itself—for example, in the great hymn "Amazing Grace" we sing, "Was blind, but now I *see*."

And not unlike the account in Mark chapter 8 of one blind man who had his eyes touched by Jesus but said he could only see people "like trees, walking" (v. 24)—one touch is not enough. It took a second touch for this man to see clearly. In reality our life with God takes not only a second touch but a third, fourth, and fifth. Our vision is regularly skewed, and we are in need of God's hand to restore our capacity to see.

God can be working all around us, but we can still lack the vision to see what He is doing. In this regard, some of us are spiritually nearsighted—anything distant is blurry. We can see what is right in front of us, but we don't have the vision to see down the line.

Others of us are spiritually farsighted. Distant objects are quite clear, but we can't see what is right under our nose with any clarity. We can get excited about the future, the grand plan, some kind of big picture—we can even be excited about what might happen five years from now. And yet at the same time, that kind of future focus keeps us from being able to see what God is doing tonight, tomorrow, and the next day. It keeps us from having crisp, clear vision at the moment we are in right now. In reality attending to what God is doing now will open the doors for what God will do in the future!

Others have spiritual color blindness. To recognize the colors and shades of God's working, the full spectrum of what God is doing in the world and inside us, requires tremendous nuance. But those who are spiritually color-blind are unable to differentiate the nuances of what God is doing. They lack this kind of careful discernment. Others have spiritual tunnel vision and are able to see one part of the picture but unable to see the periphery. They are unable to see how one small part fits into the big picture.

For all of us, spiritual vision is going to require the healing of our eyes. It is going to require new vision. We need grace-healed eyes to see ourselves and the people and places around us from a different point of view. Precisely because there are giants in the land—there are challenges and dangers that come with any new territory—we will need sharper, clearer, crisper vision than we had before. We will have to come to see with the eyes of a conqueror if we want a new normal.

07

PRAISE THAT PAVES THE WAY

When you hear them sound a long blast on the trumpets, have the whole army give a loud shout; then the wall of the city will collapse and the army will go up, everyone straight in.

JOSHUA 6:5 | NIV

I F YOU ARE beginning to wonder whether you'll ever see any battles, fear not—there are more than enough battles to be fought in this undomesticated new land! There will be no shortage of action on this new frontier. Taking this land will require consecrating ourselves and coming into this new way of seeing. There is a time and place too where we have to move forward.

The land ahead of Joshua was full of people utterly set against his intentions of taking it. There were real foes, real opponents, real enemies there. The resistance was real! And what happened to Joshua after he prayerfully discerned, listened, and came to see is what happens to all of us once we finally begin to walk into the new normal: *he hit a wall.*

Does this seem like a familiar pattern to you? Think about a time when you made a major decision to move forward with God—to kick an addiction, carve out more time for prayer and Bible study, cultivate deeper relationships with your spouse and kids, or expand your calling in some concrete way. Have you ever marched ahead without resistance? Of course not! You start moving forward, and inevitably you hit a wall. You do not pass go, and you do not collect $200.

You don't hit the wall at the end of the journey but at the beginning. The wall is not the final obstacle, generally, but the first one! Looming, intimidating, fierce—whenever you make a significant decision, you can rest assured that there is a wall already there waiting. And as it was for these people of God of old, it is not just any wall. It's *the* wall—or perhaps better said, walls.

The walls of Jericho were the first major obstacle to the people of God inhabiting this new land: "Now Jericho was shut up inside and outside because of the people of Israel. None went out, and none came in" (Josh. 6:1). In Joshua's day, Jericho was a garrison city designed to guard the land of Canaan against invasion. As such, it was a heavily fortified city with a virtually impregnable double wall. In the words of Deuteronomy 9:1, "Hear, Israel: You are now about to cross the Jordan to go in and dispossess nations greater and stronger than you, with large cities that have walls up to the sky" (NIV). Did you read that? It says *walls*, plural. And these are not modest walls, tiny walls—these are not minor hurdles to clear.

The size and scope of the walls of Jericho were staggering. Just how high were these walls? Archaeologist Kathleen Kenyon excavated the walls' remnants in the 1950s, and since then scholars have generated a schematic based on her findings that re-creates the walls accurately. Jericho had two walls—an upper wall and a lower wall. The lower wall of this two-tiered fortification system was a stone retaining wall twelve to fifteen feet high. On top of the retaining wall was a mud-brick wall six feet thick and twenty feet high. The total height of the lower wall, then, was about thirty-five feet. Then a sloped embankment went up to a second wall, an upper wall of mud-brick twenty to twenty-six feet high.[1] From the base of the lower wall to the top of the upper wall was an astonishing eighty feet. So you can understand how seemingly impossible it was for the Israelites to conquer the city!

Do you know what happened when they took in the shocking magnitude of the walls? Did they turn around and go back home? No! Joshua would be a very short book if they had never made it through these walls! Everybody knows the walls of Jericho fell. Based on the same archaeological excavations, we even know something of how they landed: the bricks from the collapsed wall created a ramp against the retaining wall so the Israelites could go straight up into the city!

But how the walls *landed* is not nearly as interesting as how the walls *fell*. And knowing how the walls fell is everything to us as we hit the wall in our lives, because the pattern set here is a constant: how these walls fall is how *all walls fall*, and how our walls will fall.

A Whole Lotta Nothing

Let's take another look at the verses that describe the beginning of the Jericho story.

> Now the gates of Jericho were securely barred because of the Israelites. No one went out and no one came in. Then the LORD said to Joshua, "See, I have delivered Jericho into your hands, along with its king and its fighting men. March around the city once with all the armed men. Do this for six days. Have seven priests carry trumpets of rams' horns in front of the ark. On the seventh day, march around the city seven times, with the priests blowing the trumpets. When you hear them sound a long blast on the trumpets, have the whole army give a loud shout; then the wall of the city will collapse and the army will go up, everyone straight in."
>
> —JOSHUA 6:1–5, NIV

We are getting to the good part where walls start falling, enemies start running, and new land becomes our land. But before the walls fall, don't miss this critical detail: what has to happen just before the walls fall, by one way of looking at it, is *a whole lotta nothing.* "March around the city once with all the armed men. Do this for six days....On the seventh day, march around the city seven times, with the priests blowing the trumpets" (vv. 3–4, NIV). OK, so before the walls fall, there is a kind of parade. Everybody loves a good parade—well, maybe once or twice a year. Marching for one day would be fine, but what about marching for six days consecutively? And marching once around the city would be OK, but what about marching around the city seven times? *Really?* Doesn't this sound a bit excessive? It hardly sounds like a military strategy!

As ready as you may be to watch the walls crumble, see the enemy flee, and occupy the city, you need to know that what immediately precedes the fall of Jericho is again what feels very much like a whole lotta nothing. You show up at the same place, at the same time, and do the same thing over and over again—and *nothing* changes.

Spoiler alert: when we, out of obedience, keep showing up to the same thing at the same time every day out of obedience, there are not always fireworks! There isn't always emotion. It's not always dramatic. It can even feel a bit like drudgery. Marching can feel long and pointless. We ask ourselves, Is this even changing anything? What am I doing here, anyway? Do I look like a fool? Everybody has those feelings when they take time to pray, read Scripture, fast, or be intentional to gather and sing in corporate worship and yet it feels as if nothing is happening.

You may feel as if it's not changing anything or making any difference at all. By the time you've marched for a few days or marched around the city almost seven times, you may well wonder, "Why even bother?" There doesn't seem to be any real strategic advantage to anything you are being asked to do. But military strategy is not the key to victory—*obedience strategy is!*

Here's the critical thing: showing up out of obedience to God in the same way at the same time and the same place *always* matters. You don't have to feel anything for it to work. Like we covered in chapter 6, you can't gauge whether the marching is successful based on what your eyes can see. You don't sit and watch the grass grow, watch the paint dry, or watch your muscles grow in the gym. You simply keep doing what has been asked of you. You keep showing up even when you don't see visible results. You keep doing what you know God told you to do, even though the feeling you had when you first heard God speak may be long gone.

Nothing changes on Sunday. Nothing changes on Monday. Nothing changes on Tuesday. Nothing changes on Wednesday. Nothing changes on Thursday. Nothing changes on Friday. Nothing changes on Saturday either—not after the first march around the city. Nor after the second. Nor after the third, the fourth, the fifth, or the sixth. It can feel long and monotonous when nothing you can see with your eyes is changing. Absolutely nothing you can see is changing—*until everything does.*

Then Comes the Shout

It is necessary in a life of faith that you show up at the same time at the same place to do the same thing. Sometimes it is even necessary to have such times when nothing visibly happens. But it is also necessary to set aside time and space for something wilder, less predictable, and more spontaneous—there has to be time and space set aside *for the shout.* Because ultimately God did not use swords to bring His people the victory. He did not use battering rams or rely on the strategy of expert military tacticians. No, the primary weapon God used was *praise*—and the sharpest point of that weapon was the *shout*!

After the monotony and routine, God *commanded* them to shout, to let go, to let everything inside them out, to move from the practice of routine obedience to the release of faith-filled praise. You can't have one without the other—the shout without the routine, or the routine without the shout. Both are equally important parts of the journey into a new land. Both are needed. But it was when they entered the complete abandon of the shout that the walls finally crumbled! The shattering of the walls is up to God. The shout is up to us!

And while the walk around the walls before may have been uneventful, the shout was anything but. According to Joshua 6:5, the shout was loud. God told Joshua to "have the whole army give a loud shout" (NIV). Again, in verse 20, we read that "the men gave a loud shout" (NIV). Volume matters to God!

> **The shattering of the walls is up to God. The shout is up to us!**

This incident in the Book of Joshua isn't isolated or obscure—this ancient pattern repeatedly happens for the people of God. The same Hebrew word we find for *shout* in Joshua is what we repeatedly find in the Psalms:

- "Clap your hands, all peoples! *Shout* to God with loud songs of joy!" (Ps. 47:1, emphasis added).

- "I *shout* in triumph" (Ps. 108:9, emphasis added).

- "Sing aloud to God our strength; *shout* for joy to the God of Jacob!" (Ps. 81:1, emphasis added).

The shout is not an optional part of life with God; the shout is essential. If you are to enter the new normal God has for you, your shouts of praise will have to get louder than the battle you are facing!

And what kind of shout was this? We know this much—the shout was celebratory. The Jews used two types of trumpets: those made of silver and those made of ram's horns. The common Hebrew word for trumpet is *shofar*; for ram's horn it is *jobel*, which is the root of the word *Jubilee*.[2] The priests used the silver trumpets to signal the camp when something important was happening (as in Numbers 10). Rams' horns, however, were used primarily for celebrations!

The priests didn't use the silver trumpets as they finished their march around Jericho, because Israel wasn't declaring war on Jericho—for there was no war. They weren't declaring war, but declaring victory! There is power in thanking God in advance of the victory. There is power in praising God before we have seen anything change. There's power in audibly, vocally celebrating what God will do. It actively builds your confidence and strengthens your faith that He is going to do it!

The sequence of the shout is equally important: the shout came *before* the victory. Joshua 6:5, again, says, "And when they make a long blast with the ram's horn, when you hear the sound of the trumpet, then all the people shall shout with a great shout, *and the wall of the city will fall down flat*" (emphasis added). And Joshua 6:20 says, "So the people shouted when the priests blew the trumpets. And it happened when the people heard the sound of the trumpet, and the people shouted with a great shout, that the wall fell down flat. *Then* the people went up into the city" (NKJV, emphasis added). The shout came before—not after—the walls came down!

> **The shout is not an optional part of life with God; the shout is essential.**

In the famous chronicle of faith heroes in Hebrews 11 the connection is explicitly made that this shout is a shout of faith. Verse 30 says, "By faith the walls of Jericho fell down after they had been encircled for seven days." For the Israelites, shouting was an act of faith! A shout of praise is always an act of faith. Praising before the victory is not ceremonial; it is a declaration that the battle has already been won! The heart of the conqueror is a heart that knows that the shout of praise can win the battle before the battle even begins.

An Altar in the Field

I'll never forget when we were getting ready to build the South campus at James River Church in 1999. We felt as if God was truly calling us to expand our ministry, and that a new and larger location to connect with more people in our community would be critical. At the time we only had a tiny fraction of what it would cost to do it in the bank. Y2K was looming large in people's minds then, and that anxiety penetrated the financial sphere. Our resources as a church were earmarked, and I simply could not see how we could take the step of building a new worship center. It felt as if our plane was on the runway but didn't have the fuel to take off.

I had been invited by Pastor Jim Cymbala to preach at the Brooklyn Tabernacle. That evening we stayed for service, and at the close Pastor Cymbala invited those with needs to come forward and worship the Lord, believing that act of faith would change their situation. As I spent that time in prayer and worship, I didn't feel anything, and I didn't hear the Lord speak anything. As we left the church and headed to the hotel, I still felt both discouraged and overwhelmed.

The next morning, I got up and boarded the flight back to Springfield. As I sat waiting for takeoff, I knew that something in me had shifted. Suddenly I saw the whole thing differently—I saw through the eyes of faith. God had done something in that evening prayer time that restored my vision even though I was unaware of it at the time. I opened my Bible and read Genesis 12, where God promised to give Abraham the land. Having received a promise that doubtless seemed impossible, Abraham built an altar and worshiped there. In that deep interior way I heard what I believe was the Spirit of God whisper to me, telling me to build an altar of praise on that new property where the new building's platform was going to be.

The next morning, I drove to the land in my pickup, and with the morning rush-hour traffic speeding by on the highway, I lifted my hands in praise and began thanking the Lord, saying, "If You say there's going to be an auditorium here, I believe You, and I will worship You." It was the shout of praise before the battle. It was the shout of faith in the face of impossibility. The shout signifies letting go of ego, letting go of attempts to intellectualize, rationalize, and work it all out, and entering into that simple trust that God will do what He promised. The shout is the move from the rational to the transrational, from giving it my best to trusting God to do what only God can do! And by the time it was all said and done, we were able to build that building as God provided the funds in ways that I never imagined possible.

You might not be called to build a new church building, but I absolutely believe there is a field of faith, a promise God has given you that on a human plane seems impossible. Only you can build an altar there. Only you can pick the rocks to signify what God has done and what you believe God will do. Only you can sing your song and play your trumpet or your air guitar! No one else can shout for you. No one else can be a substitute for your praise.

> **The shout is the move from the rational to the transrational, from giving it my best to trusting God to do what only God can do!**

God has promised that you can enter the new normal. He has prepared this place for you. You don't have to make it happen. You just have to shout for it, to praise God as if it has already happened! And the walls that once seemed insurmountable will surely crumble before the power of the living God.

PRACTICE

OK, this is a fun, simple one: praise. I know everything isn't all worked out and you don't have all the answers. I know there is still pressure and there is still conflict. But you can still praise. You can praise God for who He is, and you can give God thanks for what He has already done in your life.

Praise is a powerful spiritual force that changes the temperature in your life. What do you have to be thankful for? What is on your heart right now that makes you adore God? Take a couple of moments to jot a couple of those things down, and then take a little bit of time to offer those things to God, no matter how you feel, no matter what condition you are in. The shout is what brings the walls down!

_____

_____

_____

08

THE LAW OF FIRST THINGS

All the silver and gold and the articles of bronze and iron are sacred to the LORD and must go into his treasury.

JOSHUA 6:19 | NIV

A S THE PEOPLE of God entered the new land, Jericho was the first city they encountered. It was their opportunity to establish new patterns, set new precedents, and experience new provisions. Richard Rohr once tweeted, "How you do anything is how you do everything."[1] There is surely truth to this, but I might adapt it to say, "How you do the *first thing* is how you do everything." Because how this new land is won is how it will be sustained, and the means by which you came into it are the means by which you will attempt to occupy it.

Don't get me wrong—God is good and able to redeem all things. But especially as you feel God drawing you into a new normal and new opportunity, the way you come into this season and space has real meaning. If you have come through a season of defeat and discouragement, it's tempting to grade yourself on the curve. It's tempting to treat the first city you are called to conquer as a dress rehearsal, to tell yourself that you'll try to handle it OK this time and get it right the next time. But Jericho is not a dress rehearsal; how you handle the first stretch of new land is how you will handle *all* the land.

Don't hear this in a way that intimidates or debilitates you; the idea is not that you need to be perfectly strong, wise, or strategic. Because this land is new and unfamiliar to you, a certain amount of human bumbling is expected and not worth beating yourself up over. What God wants is not some sort of Greek ideal of perfection. God simply wants to be honored first. It is what we call the law of first things, and in the story of Scripture this is the rhythm of creation from the very beginning of time.

Before I tell you what the law of first things means, let

me tell you what it doesn't mean: it does not mean God is a greedy cosmic version of the godfather threatening to shake you down if He doesn't get His cut in time. Jesus is not standing in front of you holding an offering plate and saying in an Italian accent, "I'm gonna make you an offer you can't refuse." The law of first things is not about threats or retaliation. It's about reciprocity.

> Jericho is not a dress rehearsal; how you handle the first stretch of new land is how you will handle *all* the land.

Everything in the kingdom of God requires reciprocity: we freely receive, we freely give. Both actions require open hands. No wonder it's required that we honor God first; it's precisely in the act of giving that we open ourselves up to receive God's provision.

The Two Corollaries of the Law of First Things

The law of first things has two corollaries, and they are as follows.

1. The first part of all God gives us should be given back to Him.

God set it up this way from the beginning. It's Abel bringing the firstborn of his flock to the Lord even before there was any written law or command to tell him to do so. (See Genesis 4.) It's the ancient Israelites being told the first offspring of every womb, including the firstborn males of the livestock, belonged to God (Exod. 34:19), even the firstfruits of the ground (Exod. 34:26).

The first part has always belonged to God and still belongs to God. The first part of our paycheck belongs to God. When I get a raise, the first time the increased amount of money appears in my check, I give it all to God. For Christians this is part of what it means to worship on Sunday—a way of saying that the first part of our week belongs to God!

2. What we do with the first part determines what happens with the rest.

This principle is embedded in the narrative of Scripture over and over again. In Exodus 34:20 we read, "The first-born of a donkey you shall redeem with a lamb, or if you will not redeem it you shall break its neck." It may sound like a cryptic, violent image, but the idea is that you would be better off not to have the animal at all than to keep what is God's. Because if you keep it—if you live from a posture of clinging, holding on, being stingy, being miserly, or living from fear and control—everything is cursed. But on the other hand, when you give back to God—living from a place of release, freedom, and trust—everything is blessed!

God reinforces this promise repeatedly to His people. In Proverbs 3:9–10 He says, "Honor the LORD with your wealth and with the firstfruits of all your produce; then your barns will be filled with plenty, and your vats will be bursting with wine." It was the very founding promise God made to Israel's ancestor Abraham: "Because you have done this and have not withheld your son, your only son, I will surely bless you, and I will surely multiply your off-spring as the stars of heaven and as the sand that is on the seashore" (Gen. 22:16–17). This promise was so great, so sweeping in scope, that because Abraham did not withhold what was most dear to him, God promised that through him and his lineage all the families of the earth would be blessed (v. 18).

I just want to offer this by way of testimony—this is not empty preacher talk for me. This principle, this law of first things, is *true, true, true.* It's the kind of truth I feel in my bones. I feel urgent about it—not because I have something to gain from any of this, but because I've seen the truth of it play out consistently throughout my life.

I grew up on a farm in eastern Colorado, where three generations of Lindells made their living by sowing and reaping; therefore, none of this is abstract to me. The law of first things, which farmers would recognize as the law of the harvest, is *very* real to me. I know that if you plant one kernel of corn, you get three ears of corn; and that three ears of corn will have a minimum of six hundred kernels per ear. A farmer can literally calculate his harvest based on how much seed he plants.

So how does this principle translate to our lives? It doesn't mean everybody will drive a Ferrari, but it does mean there will be provision. Even people who are not Christians recognize this truth. From the language around the law of attraction to New Age and self-help business gurus, anybody paying attention to how the world works has to acknowledge that people reap what they sow. It almost seems counterintuitive, but those who clench their fists lose what they have; those who open their hands are able to be given more.

As I look back over my life, again and again I have watched the Lord multiply whatever I have placed in His hands. And I am not alone in this. Saints throughout the ages have understood the law of the harvest. John Bunyan, the author of the Christian classic *The Pilgrim's Progress,* wrote, "A man there was, and they called him mad; the more he gave, the more he had."[2] God can only bless what we give Him.

> **Those who clench their fists lose what they have; those who open their hands are able to be given more.**

What God asks for often doesn't make sense at the time. But that's why ultimately we cannot and should not trust our sense of the situation. The comedian and actress Anjelah Johnson tells the story of moving to Los Angeles after feeling a tug to pursue her dream of acting. But nothing was working out. She wasn't getting any auditions, leads, or parts. She had no job and no money, and she was living with family. Anjelah hilariously describes how in that season of her unmarried life, she dated because she was hungry—she literally went on dates so guys would buy her food. Being a believer, she felt as if God spoke to her that He wanted her to fast from dating and "date Him" instead. She understood that He wanted her to make spending time with Him a priority in her life.

Even though her career had completely stalled, she started getting up early every morning to pray. She would spend an hour or two reading and singing worship songs. Anjelah remembers the day she was driving down the freeway and felt butterflies in her stomach. She could only describe them as the feeling she would get when she was "feeling into a boy"—and she said out loud, "Jesus, I have such a big crush on You!"

A couple of days later she got a call from a friend who was starting an improv comedy class at the church and wanted her to participate. Anjelah asked if it was free, and her friend said yes, so she went. The assignment was to write a sketch, so she wrote her first one and titled it "Nail Salon." Someone recorded the performance of the sketch and posted it on social media. The video went viral and has since had more than forty million views. Because of it, within three months she had meetings with every major TV network and Hollywood studio and landed a gig on the final season of *MADtv*. It made no practical sense at the time. But she felt the nudge of the Spirit to put God first, above anything and anyone else. And God was faithful.

Achan's Sin

When the Israelites took Jericho, they were given explicit instructions: only Rahab (the prostitute who had hidden two of their spies) and those with her were to be spared. They were also given instruction not to take any of the articles of silver, gold, bronze, and iron, which along with expensive items of clothing were to be consecrated to the Lord and placed in the Lord's treasury (Josh. 6:16–19).

One man, Achan, decided not to comply. He was not an evil man, per se. I imagine that, like us, he was a man with bills to pay. And after such a massive victory for the entire nation he probably figured nobody would be all that bothered if he kept just a couple of things for himself. He didn't take all of the exotic treasure, just some of it—just a cloak, a few pieces of silver, and a bar of gold. It wasn't enough for anybody else to notice. It was petty theft at best. It certainly wasn't murder, in any case. At first, it reads as if it might not be more than a footnote to the story.

Later on, when his folly was exposed, it became clear

that Achan keeping these things was important enough to interfere with the favor and blessing of God resting on an entire people. But before you start booing and hissing at Achan, keep in mind that he had legitimate needs that motivated him, just as you do.

We have no idea what kind of hardship brought him into this moment. We can presume that this entire journey of coming into the land had been hard for all God's people. Don't be too quick to villainize Achan, or you won't realize how quickly you can become him. He was a guy who put his own needs above the needs of others. That's what this entire story illustrates: selfishness, greed, and holding back instead of giving back will stop the flow of God's blessing.

In shorthand we might even say it like this—Achan was a pragmatist. Jericho was full of expensive treasure, and even a little of that treasure would go a long way in paying some bills—taking some of that treasure made all the sense in the world, practically speaking. That's the trouble with thinking pragmatically. You can always justify holding on to the money. You can always justify why you need the money more than God does, more than the poor do. You can always come up with a perfectly good reason why the rule doesn't apply to you. Once again, this isn't some kind of over-the-top, overt evil. It is where limited, human-scarcity thinking gets you, instead of the kind of abundance thinking that God calls for, which would open both your hands and your heart.

As the story continues, we discover that Achan's disobedience was indeed more than a footnote. God was greatly displeased because of it. Jericho had been conquered, and next on the horizon was the city of Ai. Joshua decided to send only three thousand men to Ai after some of his scouts reported seeing only a few people there. Jericho had seemed impossible at first, but God had given them the victory. Ai looked as if it would be a cakewalk. Instead the army of Israel was routed—a disastrous defeat. Thirty-six Israelite warriors were cut down, and the rest of them were chased out of town. After the elation and jubilation of their soaring win at Jericho, the defeat completely took the life out of them. The words of the text are haunting: "And the hearts of the people melted and became as water" (Josh. 7:5).

> **Selfishness, greed, and holding back instead of giving back will stop the flow of God's blessing.**

In response to this Joshua tore his clothes and fell face-down before God until evening. It was then that God told him Israel sinned against Him by taking the devoted things and were therefore defeated. Victory would be impossible until the people of Israel gave the Lord what belonged to Him.

The image is a stark, poignant one. Again, the law of first things shows us that the first part of all God gives us should be given back to Him and that what we do with the first part determines what happens to the rest. Perhaps there was a time when you or I did not know this. But once we come to see the truth of it, we have a consequential decision to make. We must acknowledge the very real truth that as long as we think we possess anything, our possessions possess us. We do not own; we only steward. God freely gives to us, and He calls us to give back to Him freely. When we live as people who believe it all belongs to

God, we live immersed in reality, and it opens up the door for every good gift.

We ignore this principle at our peril. God's principles are not arbitrary. This principle matters because our generosity with God determines whether we will be generous with others. It determines what kind of people we will be in the world and what kind of world we will make—whether we will be closefisted people or openhanded people.

When the topic of generosity comes up, it's easy to be defensive and insist that we are only trying to look out for our needs. But a theology of scarcity (as opposed to abundance) is closely related to a theology of selfishness. And when we put ourselves first, all kinds of bad things happen. We can justify anything when we rationalize putting our needs above those of others. It's where most evil in the world begins—not with malicious intent but with people simply placing their needs above the needs of their community.

The Lasting Implications of Shortcuts

In a haunting footnote to this story Joshua pronounced, "Cursed before the LORD be the man who rises up and rebuilds this city, Jericho. At the cost of his firstborn shall he lay its foundation, and at the cost of his youngest son shall he set up its gates" (Josh. 6:26). In 1 Kings 16, during the time of the wicked King Ahab, Hiel of Bethel *did* rebuild Jericho. And in fulfillment of this mysterious verse he offered his own (likely small) children as human sacrifices, placing them dead or alive in jars and inserting them into the masonry to satisfy the pagan gods and to ward off evil spirits.

It was a vile act, to be sure. But in it we see echoes of the sin of Achan. Hiel's sin was only a more radical example of a man being willing to prioritize his own needs above the needs of others. Achan was willing to place his needs above those of his community. Hiel was willing to place his needs above those of his children. In the end, isn't it only a difference of degrees?

I get it. You might not be in a position to steal plundered treasure, much less to sacrifice your kids to ward off evil spirits. But the point is equally profound for us all: we are all given gifts. How we handle our money, our time, and our talent is important. Ultimately, God owns everything, and God provides everything. God wants the first portion of everything, and what you do with the first portion determines what happens to the rest. Of course you can choose to ignore these principles if you want to, but they are as true and as real as the law of gravity, and the implications are just as pronounced in our lives, whether we like it or not.

To conquer, we need God's help. We need God's blessing. With God's favor even the most reinforced, impenetrable city of Jericho is not impossible. Without it even the most ripe-for-the-taking, easily defeatable city of Ai is not within our grasp. God has given us His best and is always giving, giving, giving. Are you willing to open those clenched fists and give back, to give of the firstfruits? What you do with what's first will shape how you'll allow God to work with what's next.

How Do We Steal From God?

Perhaps this all sounds very heavy and dramatic—an ancient man named Achan decided the rules didn't apply to him and decided it was OK to steal from God. But if you think of Achan not as some fundamentally wicked soul but as a man who, like many of us, simply put his needs over that of the community, the story raises broader questions.

They can be uncomfortable questions: What precisely has God asked of me? What has God given me in terms of time, talents, and resources that I have squandered in the name of paying bills or meeting my own needs? How is that damaging not only me but also my community? For modern people living in Western cultures, the idea that we are somehow responsible for one another or that our lives are somehow bound together can seem strange. But ancient peoples and more Eastern cultures have always understood that none of us lives in a vacuum.

> **God wants the first portion of everything, and what you do with the first portion determines what happens to the rest.**

What we do or don't do with what God has placed in our hands has a real and lasting effect on the people around us; it can either bring blessing and abundance or a curse. The way of openness, sharing, and reciprocity is the way of the King and the way of the kingdom. If we live with open hands and open hearts, we will be blessed and open up a way of blessing for the people around us. But if we live miserly, grasping, conserving lives, only concerned about meeting the immediate needs of me and mine, that selfishness cuts off the flow of divine blessing to the people around us too.

What Achan ultimately could not grasp was that all the treasure belonged to God, that the Israelites were merely stewards of it. Is it that much different now if I decide that whatever money I make is mine to do whatever I wish without considering God or recognizing that I am part of a broader story of a people who all belong to one another? If I decide to keep back whatever I think I need instead of giving, is it not still a form of robbing God?

Achan forgot that his life was connected to others' lives and that his choices had real implications for the people around him. In contemporary Western culture we are even more likely to live with the delusion that we somehow are not responsible for one another, that we don't carry one another, and that we are not part of some kind of communal identity. But what we do with our lives and resources matters to the people around us, it matters to God, and it determines whether we experience the blessing generosity brings.

09
ASKING FOR DIRECTIONS

The Israelites sampled their provisions but did not inquire of the LORD.

JOSHUA 9:14 | NIV

THERE ARE A few complexities to coming into this new normal. Some of the challenges of coming into this new territory are more overt, more explicit. They are not necessarily easy, but at a minimum they are clear. Jericho's menacing walls force a brutal, severe sort of clarity: these walls are too high and too thick for us; we are going to have to seek a power higher than ourselves. The sin of Achan, if not massive in scale, is brazen in its way. God gave an express command that a man within the camp disobeyed, which was clearly wrong.

But the deeper we get into the land, in some ways, the more ambiguous the challenges become. It becomes increasingly difficult to tell the difference between friend and foe or opportunity and challenge. Perhaps this is the great lie: people often think that if you win one great battle, it is inevitable that you will win other great battles or even all the great battles! The reality is, clarity is a gift of the humble and hungry, and the hubris of winning a battle, even when it's God who has exclusively wrought the victory, is a very dangerous thing. As the people of God went into the land and surveyed the impenetrable city of Jericho for the first time, they were nothing if not sharp, clear, alert, and perhaps even hypervigilant. Their awareness of their weakness and inadequacy was high; their dependence on God was high.

By the time we get to Joshua 9, the Israelites were more confident—and because of that confidence, more complacent. Yes, they lost some men to Ai, but they were still savoring the victory of Jericho. They were still feeling like winners, but they weren't as hungry, sharp, or discerning as they used to be. They were not intentionally disloyal to

God and the covenant. But the pain and hunger that had caused them to be so awake to God and the world around them had been largely situated, and they were now facing the world with senses slightly more dulled than they had been before. And this made all the difference.

> **Perhaps this is the great lie: people often think that if you win one great battle, it is inevitable that you will win other great battles or even all the great battles!**

This story is especially savory because it is one of Joshua's minor stories, not the kind of headline garnered by toppling the walls of Jericho but full of color and intrigue nonetheless. The kings in the hill country and the lowland beyond Jordan had gathered to fight Joshua and Israel. But the scene shifts, and it's the inhabitants of Gibeon and Ai who have decided to act, not with brute force but with cunning. So they went out "and made ready provisions and took worn-out sacks for their donkeys, and wineskins, worn-out and torn and mended, with worn-out, patched sandals on their feet, and worn-out clothes. And all their provisions were dry and crumbly" (Josh. 9:4–5). And using brainpower instead of brawn, they set out to pull on the Israelites' collective heartstrings.

There isn't a lot of overt God-talk in the narrative, which seems to be the heart of the problem. The key verse in the whole affair is Joshua 9:14: "So the men took some of their provisions, but did not ask counsel from the LORD." Unlike the tale of Achan, there is no evidence of any direct disobedience, certainly not of any malice. There is no record here of the people of God doing anything wrong, only of what they failed to do. There was no failure of nerve, planning, or strategy—only of prayer. The whole thing turns out to be a debacle for one reason only: they failed to pray. But why? And what can this obscure ancient story teach us now?

When It Looks Too Right

First of all, if you have a hard time understanding how the Israelites could not have asked for directions at such a crucial moment, I'd suggest that you have never been lost with *a man* anywhere before! Anyone who has been lost with a man knows there is no level or degree of being lost, no matter how ridiculous or outrageous it might get, that will cause a man to make the commonsense decision to ask someone else for directions!

Beyond that the text gives us several indications as to why the Israelites didn't ask God for direction, all of which are instructive for us. The passage starts with a description of unbelievable pressure: *all* the kings beyond the Jordan gathered as one to fight Joshua and Israel. Well, that's pretty intense! Whenever there is real progress in a walk with God, whenever new ground is taken, there is always a sense that enemies gather. It can feel like some kind of cartoon, supervillain team-up! And it's not just in your head. The forces that conspire to keep you from moving forward are quite real, and the pressure applied to keep you in place is quite strong.

On paper this might seem like a great time to inquire of the Lord! But intuitively, this is not always how it works. When the pressure is on, we tend to be more reactionary than responsive. Prayer takes time and discernment. Circumstantial pressure makes us feel the need to react in real time. It seems to demand a quick response. In that moment prayer seems like a luxury we don't have; discernment seems like a privilege we cannot afford. But we need to seek God, especially when the pressure is on! When we feel the external pressure begin to crowd in on us, it clouds our discernment, fogs our gauges, and only makes our need for prayer more pronounced. The higher the pressure is turned up, the more desperately we need to seek the Lord!

> **Whenever there is real progress in a walk with God, whenever new ground is taken, there is always a sense that enemies gather.**

It may be tempting not to take time to inquire of the Lord because something looks like a good thing. On the surface everything seems right. The Gibeonites told a story that made sense. They came from a "very distant country." And why exactly had they come? "Because of the name of the LORD your God" (v. 9). After all, isn't compassion always a godly virtue? And hey, they were even able to talk that spiritual talk. What more could you hope for?

They even had evidence to back up their claims. They said, "Here is our bread. It was still warm when we took it from our houses as our food for the journey on the day we set out to come to you, but now, behold, it is dry and crumbly. These wineskins were new when we filled them, and behold, they have burst. And these garments and sandals of ours are worn out from the very long journey" (vv.

12–13). The Israelites, operating in the Homer Simpson school of discernment, basically responded with, "Mmm. This bread *does* look crumbly." The conceit of this is that the Gibeonites were from twenty-five miles away!

Sometimes the better something looks, the less we feel as if we need to seek God. The truth is, the better it looks, the *more* we need to seek God. Our senses can be so easily manipulated, especially when we are tired. We can be quick to assume something or someone is an answer to prayer just because they seem like an ideal solution at the moment. The Gibeonites said they were there "because of the name of the LORD" (v. 9). Perhaps you are single, and similar to the Gibeonites, a person who talks the spiritual talk comes along and says he or she is there because of Jesus. Perhaps you're looking for a job or a place to live, and you come across an option that seems perfect at first glance. Everything about it seems to say, "I'm here because of the Lord your God." It's easy to go with something just because it looks so right on the surface. You make a rash decision about that person, that job, or that move without ever taking the time to inquire of the Lord, without ever taking the time to ask the deeper questions—because, after all, if you can't believe your own eyes, what else can you believe?

Let's look at the deeper truth here. There is so much our physical eyes cannot see. Just because something looks right, that doesn't mean it is right. Just because someone uses "God talk," that doesn't mean they come bearing God's will. Don't be too quick to make a covenant simply because it looks like a good thing without first taking the time to inquire of the Lord.

> **Sometimes the better something looks, the less we feel as if we need to seek God. The truth is, the better it looks, the *more* we need to seek God.**

Finally, the enemies had gathered against Israel and had come to deceive them because they had heard of Israel's great success against Jericho. And this is the greatest irony of them all: whenever we experience some victory in our lives—whether it be over an addiction, a toxic relationship, or a circumstantial challenge—the temptation is to think we are now somehow uniquely safe. In reality we are never more vulnerable than we are on the other side of a fresh victory. We are tempted to be less vigilant, less self-aware, and too self-sufficient. We let our guard down as if any past victory might somehow qualify us to overcome our present challenges. That is simply not how it works.

Seeking for Your Future

Many of these battle stories in Joshua can feel very high stakes, very life-and-death. To translate them into our context now would probably feel intense—as if every single second of your existence has destiny hanging in the balance. I don't think anybody should live that way. Not every town you drive past on the highway is a Jericho for you; not every moment is of ultimate consequence. Such thinking could be paralyzing.

But I do want you to see this: even when there are decisions in your life that may not have deeply consequential implications for your life in the moment or have dramatic side effects one way or the other, I want you to keep in mind that this moment is not all there is. We are all part of a larger, broader story. And it's not just our story; it's a story that belongs to others.

Achan's sin that we looked at before had immediate, disastrous implications in the present. This story of the Gibeonites is much more nuanced and cautionary. Trusting the Gibeonites as they intentionally lied and misled was neither a wise nor good decision. But it did not result in immediate devastation. After the Gibeonites tricked the Israelites into making a covenant with them, the people of Israel were forbidden from harming them. Then "all the congregation [of Israel] murmured against the leaders" (Josh. 9:18). By the time we get to the narrative of 2 Samuel, we see that Saul and David are still wrestling with what to do with the Gibeonites.

> **In reality we are never more vulnerable than we are on the other side of a fresh victory.**

This is a final reason to seek God—so you don't damage your future. Because it's not just about this moment; it's about your legacy, about a bigger story of what God is doing in the world. Your story is not just *your* story but a larger story of a people. And to ask God for guidance at this moment is not only to trust in the present but to trust God to build a more beautiful future than you'd know how to build for yourself.

For Those Who Are Looking

We do not need to live in fear, panic, paranoia, or insecurity. We do, on the other hand, need to ask God about *everything.* We should never assume we know the answer. Presumption is our worst enemy. At James River we have made prayer our central focus because we are convinced that prayer is crucial. We aren't more spiritual, wiser, or better than anyone else. We just aim to be more dependent!

The Book of James says, "You do not have, because you do not ask" (4:2). God is eager to give us counsel, guidance, and direction. He is a communicative God who is always speaking, but we are often slow to listen.

Prayer is the key to *everything* in a life with God and beyond! If we pray, God *is* going to show us what to do. No experience, special training, or education is required; only a free and honest admission that we don't know what's next and we need God to show us. Extra-special holiness isn't asked of us; humility is. If we are willing to take the time to ask, God is always willing to answer. Directions aren't for those who are smart, just for those who are looking.

> **We are all part of a larger, broader story. And it's not just our story; it's a story that belongs to others.**

Often we are just too smart for our good. In our endless desire for knowledge and understanding, and now our seemingly endless access to information—podcasts, articles, and a plethora of online content—we outsmart ourselves. Wisdom begins when we get to the end of ourselves and realize our understanding, however well informed, is never enough, and that our deep need is to trust in something beyond ourselves. We live in a time in which we have unprecedented access to information at our fingertips. Yet it is not more information that we need but more trust. We don't need more self-dependence; we need to become more at home in our native dependence.

All too often our default is to think we know the answers, or at least to think we ought to know them. But we were meant to rely on something and someone greater than ourselves—made not just to know but to ask, to wonder, and to trust. What would it look like to stop trying to stockpile information, or even to live as if you are supposed to know the truth somehow? What would it look like to ask for directions, to admit to the limitations of our very human, often superficial way of seeing and judging on appearances and instead rely on the Spirit who knows and searches the depths of our hearts and reveals the very heart of God to us?

Even the best of us are prone to deception—especially deceiving ourselves, as unreflective and unaware as we often are of our motives. That's why discernment is such a vital word for Christians, prayerfully relying on the wisdom of the Holy Spirit to show us what we would never see in our one-dimensional way of viewing the world. There is so much we simply do not know that only God can show us. And God does not show us unless we have the humility to ask!

PRACTICE

The Book of James says, "You do not have, because you do not ask" (4:2). I am willing to bet there is some question tugging at your heart and mind even now—something that has been coming up when you lay your head on the pillow or when you are in the shower, something that is worrying you—and it may not have even crossed your mind to inquire of the Lord about. Here is the thing: if it concerns you, it concerns God, who is mindful of every detail of your life, who has numbered every hair on your head. Instead of worrying about it another moment, stuck in your head, why not just ask God about it right now? Instead of speculating, wondering, and theorizing, why not just ask and give God a chance to respond? And as a way of getting whatever question weighs on you out of your mind and handing it over, why not go ahead and write down a couple of the questions that are pressing on you the most right now?

_____

_____

_____

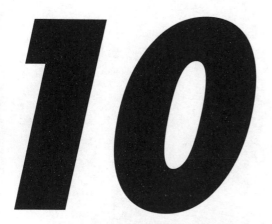

10
CRAZY-BIG REQUESTS

There has never been a day like it before or since, a day when the LORD listened to a human being. Surely the LORD was fighting for Israel!

JOSHUA 10:14 | NIV

SOMETIMES WE COME to impasses in our lives where there simply is no human solution. There are some mountains we simply cannot move. There are some problems we simply cannot resolve. There are some situations so dire and so desperate that only God can help us— where only a miracle would make a difference. Jesus taught us that God the Father is eager to give us good gifts, and I believe that miracles are among those good gifts!

At the turn of the twentieth century, tuberculosis was thought to be one of the deadliest diseases on earth, killing an estimated 450 Americans every day.[1] The diagnosis was thought to be a death sentence. So when Oscar and Paul Eliason contracted the illness in 1929, the young immigrant brothers knew the most likely outcome. The situation became hopeless when Oscar's right lung collapsed, and his brother succumbed to the disease. As Oscar grew sicker, he was confined to bed, was plagued with depression, and became certain his death was imminent. He asked a visiting pastor to pray for him and was miraculously healed.[2]

Two years later he opened up the Minneapolis *StarTribune* to find an ad from the construction company that dug the Panama Canal.[3] Their slogan, using the words of a poem sung by the workmen on the canal, caught his attention: "We specialize in the wholly impossible, doing things 'nobody ever could do.'"[4] He knew the advertisement didn't have it right and thought, "Only God can say that!" With those words serving as his inspiration, he wrote the chorus "Got Any Rivers." [5] If you aren't familiar, the lyrics talk about God specializing in doing the very things we think are impossible. Now and then during my quiet time with the Lord I find myself spontaneously singing the lines of this hymn. They are a reminder of a powerful truth: God does miracles!

Every August our church does twenty-one days of fasting and prayer because we know that some things will not happen unless we fast and pray. The theme for our fast in 2020 was "Mountains Will Move." In the middle of the fast I was diagnosed with prostate cancer. It didn't catch me by surprise, because my PSA level had gradually increased. For those not familiar with the term PSA, the letters don't stand for "Public Service Announcement" but for "prostate-specific antigen." It is one means of discerning if a man has prostate cancer. With my PSA number gradually increasing, my doctor had suggested a biopsy, and the results came back positive for cancer. Because the church was fasting and praying, I knew I wanted them to join me in praying for the mountain of cancer to move, and I believed God was going to do something supernatural in response to our prayers.

As we made the announcement asking them to pray, an interesting thing happened. I couldn't stop smiling! I felt a joy in my heart like I had never felt before. The Lord opened the door for me to participate in a clinical trial that involved a new approach to treating prostate cancer. Within two weeks of having my biopsy, I was cancer-free and was back preaching at James River Church. The Lord had moved the mountain, but even more, during those two weeks, both Debbie and I experienced a joy we had never known in our entire lives. It was a reminder that God can move mountains, but He does even more than move mountains! If mountains need to be moved in your life, remember there is a God who delights in doing the impossible—and even more!

The Sun Stands Still

Remember we move from glory to glory. It is the nature of the life of faith for each test to strengthen and prepare us for the challenges that lie ahead. There was a time, after the seemingly endless years of wilderness wandering, that the people of God could have never imagined crossing over the mighty river Jordan into the Promised Land. Even after they had crossed over, surely it would have been inconceivable for many of them to imagine taking the legendary city of Jericho. With each test they were learning to trust God in deeper, fuller ways. They were slowly gaining confidence—not in their abilities but in the good character of the God who had called them.

At every turn God was faithful to deliver them. At every turn their enemies were defeated. But Joshua's plot builds like one of our contemporary superhero tales, defeating one villain, then another—to a whole rogues' gallery of villains! Think about the old *Batman* TV show in the sixties, when the Joker, Penguin, Catwoman, and the Riddler would all team up to take on Batman and Robin.

As Israel's army became more and more feared, five kings united to overtake Gibeon because Gibeon had made peace with the people of God. It was the ultimate test for a people newly minted in battle, now forced to take on not one but five formidable foes who plotted against them. Once again, the Lord went before them. Before a single battle was fought, God threw the enemy into a panic, and more enemy soldiers were killed by mysterious hailstones that fell from heaven than were killed with the sword (Josh. 10:11).

Yet it was after this that the most extraordinary thing happened, a truly mind-boggling event never again to be duplicated in Scripture. "Joshua spoke to the LORD...and he said in the sight of Israel, 'Sun, stand still at Gibeon, and moon, in the valley of Aijalon.' And the sun stood still, and the moon stopped, until the nation took vengeance on their enemies" (vv. 12–13).

It boggles the mind to imagine a scene in which the laws of science are suspended in response to one man's prayer. "There has been no day like it before or since, when the LORD heeded the voice of a man, for the LORD fought for Israel" (v. 14). Even this description carries a trace of understatement. How could there ever be such a day to compare to this?

When he was Moses' lowly assistant, Joshua could have scarcely imagined leading his people over the Jordan River. Yet by this point in the story he was so fully convinced of the goodness and faithfulness of God that he made a request so audacious it seemed almost comical: he requested that the sun stand still, that the stars and elements themselves would bend to the power of the living God.

This was not arrogance or hubris—this was the natural expression of a man growing accustomed to seeing God bend the rules of possibility. His faith was slowly becoming larger, more spacious, and more audacious to make room for the vastness of his God. Joshua had seen God do it too many times. He knew now that nothing was impossible for God, and he spoke and acted from that place of deep conviction. Not only did the sun stand still, but all five kings were defeated. By way of epilogue the Book of Joshua records, "So Joshua took the whole land," and then beauti-fully adds, "And the land had rest from war" (11:23).

What do we make of such exploits? Gradually throughout the Book of Joshua we see Joshua's faith (and the faith of his people) grow, until ultimately there was nothing he would not ask, and nothing he would not believe his God could do! When a person comes to know and trust God in this way, nothing is impossible, and nothing is unimaginable. There are no limits to a life lived from this kind of deep, abiding trust.

I don't know what circumstance you are facing right now or how impossible it might feel. But I know what it is to feel surrounded, as if you face not one but five enemy armies, and there is trouble on every side. I know what it is to exhaust every natural, reasonable option in front of you, only to have things get exponentially worse instead of better. I know the despair and discouragement that can set in when you have done everything you know how to do, and yet nothing changes.

But I also know the God who can make the very sun stand still, who is willing to arrest time itself to come to our aid. I know that this God answers prayer and loves to give good gifts to His children. Jesus said:

> Ask and it will be given to you; seek and you will find; knock and the door will be opened to you. For everyone who asks receives; the one who seeks finds; and to the one who knocks, the door will be opened. Which of you, if your son asks for bread, will give him a stone? Or if he asks for a fish, will give him a snake? If you, then, though you are evil, know how to give good gifts to your children, how much more will your Father in heaven give good gifts to those who ask him!
> —MATTHEW 7:7–11, NIV

Pause to breathe in those words for just a moment. Let them fill you up. Can you *feel* the truth of these words?

God loves to give His kids good gifts; He is on pins and needles just waiting for you to *ask*. Nothing, absolutely nothing you will ever ask is too difficult for God to do, and there are no lengths to which He is unwilling to go to demonstrate the depths of His love for you.

It sounds painfully simple, but I believe it comes down to this: God is waiting for us to ask. God is waiting for a woman or man with the hope, fire, trust, and audacity to ask for something outrageous, to recognize that our rules do not bind Him. Making the sun stand still wasn't meant to be a one-off moment in history, but a moment to embody the all-encompassing power of God that is always available to God's daughters and sons at any place and time in history! These miracles, too, are part of the order of the new normal. Whatever you are thinking of right now, the thing you are almost afraid to ask—it may be big, but I promise you, it's not too big for God.

> Nothing, absolutely nothing you will ever ask is too difficult for God to do, and there are no lengths to which He is unwilling to go to demonstrate the depths of His love for you.

PRACTICE

This one shouldn't take you long because it's not something you have to dig for. It's right there beneath the surface—the thing you desperately want God to do but are afraid to ask because it seems too big or you don't feel worthy enough. Right now, put all that aside and remember how much God loves to give good gifts to His children, how much God delights in answering prayer. Now, what is your one crazy-big request? Write it down.

_____

_____

_____

FULL-ON

So Hebron has belonged to Caleb son of Jephunneh the Kenizzite ever since, because he followed the Lord, the God of Israel, wholeheartedly.

JOSHUA 14:14 | NIV

THE OLD MAN rose, his skin like leather from the Middle Eastern sun. The lines and creases on his face told stories without using words, yet a hush fell over the crowd for the words his mouth would tell. Some say father time remains undefeated, but the hope in this man's gaze and the faint strut in his gait seemed somehow youthful and defiant. While he wore his years, they rolled off easily when he spoke, and you could imagine him as a man of forty, walking with Joshua to explore the land for the first time. That same wonder, that same innocence, still danced like fire in his eyes.

He spoke softly at first, but his voice grew more thunderous the more he spoke. He told about how they brought back that first report of the land, and how his brothers melted with fear. But then he said, "I, however, followed the LORD my God *wholeheartedly*" (Josh. 14:8, NIV, emphasis added), and even the largest men in the crowd shivered from the electricity in those words. Yes, something else entirely came out of Caleb when he talked about his devotion to his God, and it still shook the ground just to speak of it. He told of how Moses himself swore to him on the spot that the land would be his inheritance forever because he had followed the God of Israel wholeheartedly. And again, the electricity in the air let you know that Caleb's heart still burned for his God.

Caleb testified how God had kept His promise, building to a crescendo: "So here I am today, eighty-five years old! I am still as strong today as the day Moses sent me out; I'm as vigorous to go out to battle now as I was then" (Josh. 14:10–11, NIV). At that point the sound of tears in the crowd was audible. The power of the old man's faith, the rigor of his dedication, and the sheer scope of his testimony stunned everyone.

And yet this was not the sentiment of an old man riding off into the sunset, remembering the good old days of yesteryear, wistfully paying final homage to the past. The fire that animated him then still burned in him now, and the desire to see God's promises come to pass was as bright and clear in him as ever. He said, "Now give me this hill country of which the LORD spoke on that day, for you heard on that day how the Anakim were there, with great fortified cities. It may be that the LORD will be with me, and I shall drive them out just as the LORD said" (Josh. 14:12).

I imagine the crowd on its feet whooping, shouting, and applauding as he said these words. Caleb was not some old-time mascot; his faith was leading them, and God was moving through him. He didn't come just for the speech; he came for the land. This man was ready for action one more time. He wasn't willing to stop until he saw everything God had promised come to pass.

And why? Because he followed the Lord wholeheartedly. Caleb is never described as bigger or stronger than anyone else; we have no description of him being a superior strategist or charismatic leader. He wasn't brimming with any special gifts or talents that we know of, but he had a heart that he was willing to give fully to his God—and that made all the difference.

As far as we know, the area Caleb would take as his home was the last region of the Promised Land to be inhabited by giants. Yet Caleb's wholehearted devotion resulted in words filled with faith: "It may be that the LORD will be with me, and I shall drive them out" (Josh. 14:12). The Bible doesn't describe Caleb's fight with the giants, because it wasn't Caleb's strength that conquered them. All Caleb had to do was decide that he was going to follow God wholeheartedly. The product of that decision was words of incredible faith and supernatural help from God. When it comes to entering a new normal, we can't waste time worrying about giants. What matters most is having a heart that's undivided in its devotion to God.

Extra Heart

It's been popular among teenagers in the last few years to describe people as either "basic" or "extra." To be *basic* is to be simple, without complexity or substance. *Extra* can be used to describe excess in fashion, attitude, or personality. While God is not looking for people with extra talent, ability, charisma, or resources, when it comes to heart, God is always looking for *extra*. God loves big, wholehearted, full-on devotion. God loves it when people hold nothing back and give without reserve of their whole, deepest, truest selves.

We talk a lot in church circles about wanting more of God, but truthfully, all of God is always accessible to God's sons and daughters. We can have as much of God—His presence and goodness—as we want. That is never in question. God loves to give good gifts to His children! The issue is not us getting more of God but *God getting more of us*. Are we willing to let go of every inhibition that has held us back before? Are we willing to be completely devoted, free from every hesitation? Are we willing to be *uninhibited*?

When the Book of Joshua introduces Caleb, being wholehearted is the one thing he is known for. It is the characteristic for which the ancient Hebrew tradition will forever remember him. Scripture says the same thing about him every time: he followed the Lord *wholeheartedly*. Numbers 14:24 frames it this way, "But because my servant Caleb *has a different spirit and follows me wholeheartedly*, I will bring him into the land he went to, and his descendants will inherit it" (NIV, emphasis added).

> **While God is not looking for people with extra talent, ability, charisma, or resources, when it comes to heart, God is always looking for *extra*.**

We live in a time in which nearly everyone in our culture is obsessed with being different, finding their niche, and figuring out what will make them stand out. It doesn't matter if you're in middle school or middle management, on social media or socializing at a party—everybody wants to find what sets them apart. Whether it's a haircut, a quirky car, a foreign film collection, a college football team, or a genre of music, there are countless things we can find to define us as different. Of course there is nothing inherently wrong with self-expression, but the relentless pursuit of it as a tool to define us can be nothing less than exhausting. The pursuit of self-expression becomes relentless precisely because we look to external things to tell us (and others) who we are.

Not so with God! As Scripture tells us, "Man looks on the outward appearance, but the LORD looks on the heart" (1 Sam. 16:7). God isn't interested in hairstyles or hobbies; God is interested in your heart. God doesn't need more stuff; God needs more *you*. God wants more of what is inside. It is your heart that fascinates Him. He longs for what's inside you. So many people in your life make you feel as if you need to be smarter, savvier, more beautiful, more this, or more that. God doesn't want anything in this world—except *more of you*.

Touring the Land vs. Possessing the Land

A lot of people will glimpse the land, the new normal, like a tourist. Many will fly over. Some will even occasionally visit. The land will haunt their dreams. They will almost taste the milk and honey from their pillows, almost feel the lush vegetation of this exotic place from the safety of their beds. And yet most people will only view the land from a distance. They will see God working in someone else's life and imagine it as their own.

The issue is not us getting more of God but *God getting more of us.*

But if you don't come into the new normal, it won't be because you don't have the natural gifts or ability. It won't be because you weren't the best or brightest. It won't be about natural selection or survival of the fittest. It won't even be because you weren't tough enough. It will be because you weren't willing to pay the price of total commitment. Unfulfilled dreams and unsatiated desires will always characterize a life of halfhearted commitment.

Desire, contrary to popular opinion, is not a dirty word. God longs to "give you the desires of your heart" (Ps. 37:4). But for our desires to be trusted, we have to commit our hearts to God first. Doing this creates boundaries for our desires, causing us to desire what is best for us and what God desires for us. When we commit ourselves fully to God, we will want what God wants for us because we trust that what God wants is always good.

> **Unfulfilled dreams and unsatiated desires will always characterize a life of halfhearted commitment.**

After all, God desires that we would possess the land—not a part or piece of the land but all of it. God wants us to be spiritually, emotionally, and psychologically whole. God wants to bring us into the new normal, where our relationships are at peace and we have favor in our work. Everywhere we go, everywhere our feet touch, we bring the grace of God with us. The rule and reign of heaven come to earth until the prayer that followers of Jesus have been praying for two thousand years is finally fulfilled: "Your kingdom come, your will be done, on earth as it is in heaven" (Matt. 6:10).

God has always been interested in *land*, in earth, in real life. That's why the prophet Isaiah prophesied that the day would come when "the earth shall be full of the knowledge of the LORD as the waters cover the sea" (Isa. 11:9). Paul said the earth itself is groaning for the restoration that is coming. And we are the ones that bring that kind of healing and change to the earth—to the land!

That may sound grandiose, but it starts right here, right now, right where you are. It starts on this land, this place, wherever you are reading right now. This chair or couch. This desk or office. This coffee shop or park bench. This car, bus, train, or plane. The good reign of God needs to be right here with you. You have the opportunity to submit to God, to be wholehearted to God right here.

> **The heart of a conqueror is simply a heart handed over to the God who formed it.**

You already have everything you need, because you have your whole self. You have your whole heart. Whatever you have kept back for yourself, are you willing to hand it over? Are you willing to be wholehearted? You aren't born with the heart of a conqueror. The heart of a conqueror is simply a heart handed over to the God who formed it. And when we allow the Lord to have His way in our hearts, we can be sure that a new normal is right around the corner.

12

LIVING FOR LEGACY

But as for me and my household, we will serve the LORD.

JOSHUA 24:15 | NIV

IKE THE OLD man Caleb, Joshua lived to see God do extraordinary things in his life and the lives of the people he loved. He occupied the land and saw the walls of Jericho fall. He saw God do the impossible over and over again. But Joshua's story, like all great stories, would ultimately come to an end. So as he prepared to trust the same God to cross over one more river—not the Jordan this time but the one from this world into the next— he reflected on his life and legacy. Seasoned now from the years of struggle, he gathered the tribes of Israel for one last charge. In a remarkable final address he distilled the wisdom of an undomesticated life full of conquest and battles down to a simple, clear, final challenge. In short, he threw down the gauntlet.

> Now therefore fear the LORD and serve him in sincerity and in faithfulness. Put away the gods that your fathers served beyond the River and in Egypt, and serve the LORD. And if it is evil in your eyes to serve the LORD, choose this day whom you will serve, whether the gods your fathers served in the region beyond the River, or the gods of the Amorites in whose land you dwell. But as for me and my house, we will serve the LORD.
> —JOSHUA 24:14–15

If Caleb's rousing account of God's faithfulness in his advanced years felt like a kind of rallying cry, Joshua's charge, while no less inspiring, leaves us both a challenge and a cautionary note. Joshua and Caleb's generation lived to see the faithfulness of God, and they assure us that God will continue to fulfill His promises and honor His word. But we don't choose to serve God in a vacuum. To serve the God of Abraham, Isaac, and Jacob always puts us in immediate conflict with other gods, with other "principalities" and "powers" in the language of the apostle Paul. (See Ephesians 6:12.) We cannot serve God and also serve the lesser gods that compete for our love and loyalty. We will have to make a decision.

You will have to make a decision; no one else can make it for you.

Like with Caleb's stirring testimony, you can feel the fire coming off these ancient words of Joshua's even now. You can feel the heat and the passion in them. That simple, humble, confessional-but-powerful declaration of Joshua's choice—the choice he made as a young man and reaffirmed every day of his life—was the same choice he actively made all over again knowing his life was nearly over. Joshua was saying, "I don't know what *y'all* are going to do, but I'm going to tell you right now what my family and I are going to do: we are going to the serve the Lord!"

On one level, every generation will have moments to take responsibility for their story. Everybody comes to the moment when they must decide if they will take their place in the ongoing story of God and His people and enter the new normal. But Joshua wisely understood that his story was part of a broader story, a story of a people. His story had real implications for the real lives of people around him—his family, friends, and community. And there is a very real way in which men and women of God have to acknowledge how deeply connected our lives are, and yes, take responsibility for the stories of others. We cannot ultimately control the choices of the people around us. But whether we choose to live faithfully will profoundly affect the shape and character of their journeys.

Other Gods

The call in Joshua 24:14 is, "Fear the LORD and serve him in sincerity and in faithfulness. Put away the gods that your fathers served." The Hebrew word *tamim*, translated as "sincerity," connotes the idea of wholeness, blamelessness, and even perfection.[1] The idea is not some static state of sinlessness or coming to a place of spirituality where you are somehow beyond improvement. Rather, Joshua is making a passionate plea for full devotion—or, to use this word again, that the people would be utterly *wholehearted* in their worship of God. The sincerity or perfection he is calling for isn't moralism but white-hot love.

There's a reason the man most associated with the doctrine of holiness in church history, John Wesley, often spoke of sanctification (being set apart for God) simply as being made perfect in love. For Wesley, a holy life was simply a life where one's heart was given fully to God with nothing held back.

Even people who had seen God do these breathtaking miracles needed to hear this because the people of God have always struggled with divided loyalties. They worshiped gods other than the true God back when they were slaves in Egypt, like the goat demons mentioned in Leviticus 17 and the demons in the wilderness in Deuteronomy 32. Even in this new land of Canaan, full of promise and opportunity, some were already worshiping the Amorite gods. They had never totally rid themselves of false gods.

It reminds us that it is entirely possible for people to have godly leadership, be on the adventure of conquering new land, enjoy God's provision, and see miracles but still have divided loyalty when it comes to their God. It is not that they don't want God, per se—they just want their other gods too.

But here's what the older, wiser Joshua knew from years of watching this cycle of obedience and rebellion: if they did not make a conscientious, intentional, deliberate choice to exclusively, passionately, wholeheartedly serve the living God, and get rid of all their idols, then eventually they would serve those idols more than they would serve God.

The term *idolatry* may sound foreign and exotic to contemporary ears, conjuring images of obscure, ancient statues. But there are idols all around us, and we continually make idols out of things in our lives. Many if not most of them are not inherently bad things. Idols are mostly good things that become bad for us precisely because our affections for them become displaced, and we attempt to use them to fulfill and satisfy us in ways that they simply cannot. Family—or our ideal of a family—can become an idol; a job or career can become an idol. So can health, our appearance, money, possessions, or a political party. None of these things are intrinsically evil, but they become unhealthy when they are the object of our worship.

> **Idols are mostly good things that become bad for us precisely because our affections for them become displaced, and we attempt to use them to fulfill and satisfy us in ways that they simply cannot.**

Even when people turn to destructive and addictive behaviors such as drugs, alcohol, food, sexual sin, or pornography, they attempt to meet a legitimate need in an illegitimate, unhelpful way. Our loneliness and longing, our deep need for intimacy, acceptance, and fulfillment, are very real, and God fully intends to satisfy these longings. The trouble with our idols is that they lie to us about what they can deliver. They cannot fulfill these longings, and instead leave us empty. They make promises to us that they cannot keep. Only God can.

The best way to know if something has become an idol for you is to learn to listen to your heart. What do you treasure? What do you cherish? What brings you the most joy? What do you most fear losing? What can't you let go of? What are you holding on to a little too tightly? What has become necessary to bring you relief? Work can be an object of worship in its own way. But if you have to party, surf the internet, or masturbate to find comfort, what is your life saying to you? If you want to know where your idols are, the place you go for comfort is often the first place to look.

The Power of a Choice

As we've seen in this account of Joshua's life and times, different kinds of battles must be fought, and different kinds of cities must be taken. There is no simple, one-size-fits-all strategy for victory, which is why a life with God requires constant, real-time dependence and trust. You will never read one book that will give you all the answers or hear one sermon and get it all down. There will always be new challenges and opportunities that will require you to expand your faith and trust God differently. But no matter where you are on the journey now, where you've been, or where you are headed, I can tell you this much: what happens next starts with a simple choice.

Intention is no small thing. Deciding which direction to go or choosing whom you will serve is no small thing. Deciding whether you are going to live wholeheartedly is *the* decision that changes everything. Strategies may change from one season to the next. God will make Himself known to you in different ways from one season to the next. The diversity of how God meets with you, the surprise of God, makes life such an adventure! But choosing to serve the Lord with your whole self is the next right thing from wherever you are.

There is power in making a choice. And it's not just power for you. You make choices that affect your kids. You make choices that affect your friends. You make choices that affect your community, because all our lives are connected. God built us this way. And the best way for you to serve them well is to serve Him with everything you have and everything you are.

The ancient Israelites took the responsibility of passing down the legacy from one generation to the next very seriously.

> These are the commands, decrees and laws the LORD your God directed me to teach you to observe in the land that you are crossing the Jordan to possess, *so that you, your children and their children after them may fear the LORD your God as long as you live* by keeping all his decrees and commands that I give you, and so that you may enjoy long life. Hear, Israel, and be careful to obey so that it may go well with you and that you may increase greatly in a land flowing with milk and honey, just as the LORD, the God of your ancestors,

promised you. Hear, O Israel: The LORD our God, the LORD is one. Love the LORD your God with all your heart and with all your soul and with all your strength. These commandments that I give you today are to be on your hearts. *Impress them on your children. Talk about them when you sit at home and when you walk along the road, when you lie down and when you get up. Tie them as symbols on your hands and bind them on your foreheads. Write them on the doorframes of your houses and on your gates.*
—DEUTERONOMY 6:1–9, NIV, EMPHASIS ADDED

The expectation was to tell the story of the faith. Tell *your* story of the faith. Tell your testimony. Talk about it all the time. Keep it in front of people, when they come and when they go. Let the story of God, the story of your people, be the guiding story of your family. Find yourself in it; find your place in it together.

> **While it is not within your jurisdiction to right every wrong or address every evil, you have been given influence over a particular people in a particular place. What you do with your life— what you choose to do with your heart—makes all the difference.**

The Book of Judges tells a story of a darker time in Israel's history, after Joshua and the elders who outlived him were gone, when the people of God lost the plot. The description is sobering: "And there arose another generation after them who did not know the LORD or the work that he had done for Israel" (Judg. 2:10). We are always just one generation away from forgetting, from losing the story. The story of the faith has been passed down to us. It roots us in the story of God's faithfulness and tethers us to a narrative of His goodness. It's a story worth preserving. It's a story through which we can make sense of our lives, through which we can make sense of the world, as chaotic as it may be.

While it is not within your jurisdiction to right every wrong or address every evil, you have been given influence over a particular people in a particular place. What you do with your life—what you choose to do with your heart—makes all the difference. Yes, there are giants in the land. Yes, there are walls around the city. There are false gods to allure you around every corner. But amid the dangers and temptations, the God who called Joshua calls out to you now: there is a new normal for you to occupy too. There is a place where you belong. You have a place in the story of God and the story of God's people. There are adventures and exploits beyond your reckoning that already have your name on them. There are victories God is eager to win for you. And although there are many things about your life that you may not be able to control, your heart is decidedly not one of them.

Choose you this day whom you will serve.

EPILOGUE

And Joshua recorded these things in the Book of the Law of God. Then he took a large stone and set it up there under the oak near the holy place of the LORD.

JOSHUA 24:26 | *NIV*

JOSHUA REMEMBERED THE days before it all happened, before saying yes to the God of his fathers opened him to adventures wilder than he could have even imagined as a boy. He remembered what it was like to catch his first glimpse of the land as a spy, a pilgrim. There was a time when he too was only a visitor to the land of promise. Many had seen it. Some had passed through there. But what set Joshua apart, even in his youth, was that visiting was not enough. He had the restlessness of belief, the kind of sacred discontent that cannot be satiated until you've seen God bring something to pass with your own eyes. He had a righteous stubbornness that would not yield to the cynicism of the people around him. There was no way he could have *known* what lay ahead—but he chose to *believe*.

So after giving his final admonition to his people to serve the God who had never failed him, there was only one thing left for the old man to do. The physical agility he had when he first snuck into the land as a young man was gone, but the fire he felt inside was still ablaze. After making a final covenant with the people, as they reaffirmed their loyalty to the living God, the old Joshua sat down and began to write. His hand didn't feel frail as he remembered the stories of how God made every dream into reality, how every hope was delivered full term. He wrote in the book of the law of God and then straightened his creaking back as he went to pick up a large stone and set it under the oak next to the sanctuary of the Lord. His life was a testament to faith, fidelity, courage, and keeping promises. Those last words he wrote down, and that one last rock, would be final markers to a life well lived, and most of all, to the God who was faithful to do everything He ever said He would do. For the rest of Joshua's days the people served the Lord.

Whether or not you ever write it down, the story of your life is being written. There is a rock that will testify of your legacy after you're gone. It doesn't matter what mistakes you made before—there is a land that stretches before you now, full of God-sized opportunity and adventure. There is nothing you can do about what has gone before. But there is an opening to trust the God of Joshua here and now, with your story and your battles. I know there are giants in the land. I know some walls seem impenetrable. But Joshua and Caleb and a whole host of elders call out through the ages, beckoning us to join the company of those who have believed in the promise and the Promise Keeper for a new normal.

Fearlessness is not required. Faith is. Do you have faith that is willing to start taking steps now toward what God has for you, even though you don't have all the answers? Are you willing to take the next step, even though the very step after that has not yet been given? Do you have faith that doesn't know the end of the story but trusts the heart of the One who put the story in motion and is faithful to bring you across the finish line?

A new normal awaits you. There are many uncertainties about the road ahead. But you know in your gut that there is no going back to the world you have known before, and you know you can't stand still. The same God who led Joshua says, "I will be with you wherever you go." *He not only invites you to visit the land of blessing but offers the strength and wisdom to live in it*!

ACKNOWLEDGMENTS

T HIS BOOK WOULD not exist without God generously surrounding me with people who have been invaluable partners in this project. I am incredibly grateful to every person who has played a part in seeing this book take shape, but I want to specifically thank the following people for their help along the way.

Thank you to the people of James River Church, who have continually prayed for me and encouraged me with their faith and faithfulness. It is my joy to be your pastor!

Thank you to the team at Charisma House, which has been a delight to work with and a wonderful help in so many ways through the process of bringing this book to print.

Thank you to Jonathan Martin, who helped me craft this content to make the truths in it come alive for every person who picks it up.

And thank you to my wife, Debbie, who is a constant inspiration and the love of my life!

NOTES

1. To contemporary ears the conquest language
of the Joshua narrative can feel harsh, and
culturally and politically problematic. But keep
in mind that for the earliest Christians—the
followers of Jesus in the first few centuries
after He lived, died, and resurrected; the people
closest to the time and culture of Jesus—those
early fathers of the church were quick to use
these stories to talk not just about geographical
land but about the land that needed to be taken
in us. They were unafraid when reading about
ancient Amalekites who warred against the
people of God, to reflect on the Amalekites *in
them,* as a way of speaking of spiritual warfare.
The Spirit inspired them to use the battles
within this text in a way that was analogous
to their battles. In other words, they were
unafraid to find the universal application in this
very particular story. (It is also worth noting
that nearly all the early church fathers, from
the Epistle of Barnabas to Justin Martyr, to
Tertullian to Origen, to Eusebius to Cyril, to
Zeno of Verona and Augustine of Hippo, to the
great early translator Jerome, saw Jesus Christ

Himself prefigured in the person and work of Joshua!)

Because they understood that this wasn't just a story about history, but about the present. That this wasn't just a story about external opponents, but inward ones. They understood that the foes we needed to conquer to enter the land we ourselves had been promised weren't just historical, but spiritual—*current, real, active.* They give us permission to enter Scripture as a kind of time machine, where the battles of the present are caught up in the battles of the past and of the future, where the stories of Joshua aren't stale stories in a history book meant to be memorized but active stories of a living book in which we can find ourselves!

2. The George Müller Charitable Trust, "Timeline," accessed October 31, 2020, https://www.mullers.org/timeline.

3. Charles Inglis, "Mr. Müller and the Fog," accessed October 31, 2020, Mullers.org/find-out-more-1875.

4. Inglis, "Mr. Müller and the Fog."

5. Inglis, "Mr. Müller and the Fog."

6. Inglis, "Mr. Müller and the Fog."

7. Inglis, "Mr. Müller and the Fog."

Chapter 2

1. Henry David Thoreau, *Walden* (Boston: James R. Osgood and Company, 1878), 10.

Chapter 3

1. Dwight D. Eisenhower, *Dwight D. Eisenhower, 1957*, Public Papers of the Presidents of the United States (Washington, DC: Federal Register Division, National Archives and Records Service, General Services Administration, 1934), 818, https://babel. hathitrust.org/cgi/pt?id=miua.4728417.1957.001 &view=1up&seq=858.

2. StudyLight.org, s.v. "*kadesh*," accessed October 31, 2020, https://www.studylight.org/lexicons/ hebrew/06946.html.

3. Bob Goff (@bobgoff), "The way we deal with uncertainty says a lot about whether Jesus is ahead of us leading, or behind us just carrying our stuff," Twitter, November 1, 2017, 8:32 a.m., https://twitter.com/bobgoff/ status/925702079716384768.

4. In the words of the poet Elizabeth Barrett Browning, "Earth's crammed with heaven, and every common bush afire with God." That's the part of her 1856 poem "Aurora Leigh" that people have most often heard. But the second part of the stanza is equally important: "But only he who sees, takes off his shoes, the rest sit round it and pluck blackberries." It's a brilliant line, because indeed every bush *is* afire with God, and the wonder, the glory, the supernatural is all around us! But to see it, to experience it, takes intentionality. To "sit and take off your shoes" is an act of *consecration*.

5. Walter Brueggemann, *The Land: Place as Gift, Promise, and Challenge in Biblical Faith* (Philadelphia: Fortress Press, 1977) 45, accessed October 31, 2020, http://preachingsource.com/journal/theological-themes-in-the-book-of-joshua/.

Chapter 4

1. Tommy Caldwell, *The Push* (New York: Viking, 2017).
2. Caldwell, *The Push*; Hayden Carpenter, "What 'The Dawn Wall' Left Out," Outside, September 18, 2018, https://www.outsideonline.com/2344706/dawn-wall-documentary-tommy-caldwell-review.
3. William Shakespeare, *As You Like It, The Arden Shakespeare: Third Series*, ed. Juliet Dusinberre (London: Bloomsbury Publishing, 2006), 227.

Chapter 5

1. Blue Letter Bible, s.v. *"Gilgal,"* accessed October 31, 2020, https://www.blueletterbible.org/lang/Lexicon/Lexicon.cfm?strongs=H1537&t=KJV.

Chapter 7

1. Bryant Wood, "The Walls of Jericho," *Creation* 21, vol. 2 (March 1999): 36–40.
2. Dave Roos, "How the Rolling Jubilee Works," How Stuff Works, December 10, 2012, https://money.howstuffworks.com/personal-finance/debt-management/rolling-jubilee1.htm.

Chapter 8

1. Richard Rohr (@RichardRohrOFM), "How you do anything is how you do everything," Twitter, February 4, 2015, 10:45 a.m., https://twitter.com/RichardRohrOFM/status/563000431329435650.

2. Tryon Edwards, *A Dictionary of Thoughts* (Detroit: F. B. Dickerson Company, 1902), 191, https://www.google.com/books/edition/A_Dictionary_of_Thoughts/2GxBAQAAMAAJ?hl=en&gbpv=1.

Chapter 10

1. "Early Research and Treatment of Tuberculosis in the 19th Century," University of Virginia, accessed October 31, 2020, http://exhibits.hsl.virginia.edu/alav/tuberculosis/.

2. Glenn Gohr, "Got Any Rivers?," *Assemblies of God Heritage* 16, no. 4 (Winter 1996–97): 9.

3. Gohr, "Got Any Rivers?"

4. Berton Braley, "At Your Service: The Panama Gang" published in *Collier's Weekly*, May 31, 1913, accessed October 31, 2020, https://www.bertonbraley.com/at_your_service__the_panama_gang.htm.

5. Gohr, "Got Any Rivers?"

Chapter 12

1. Bible Hub, s.v. "*tamim*," accessed October 31, 2020, https://biblehub.com/hebrew/8549.htm.